W9-DGV-133

Mixed Heritage

Other Books in the Social Issues Firsthand Series:

Mixed Heritage

Stefan Kiesbye, Book Editor

GREENHAVEN PRESS
A part of Gale, Cengage Learning

Detroit • New York • San Francisco • New Haven, Conn • Waterville, Maine • London

Christine Nasso, *Publisher*
Elizabeth Des Chenes, *Managing Editor*

© 2009 Greenhaven Press, a part of Gale, Cengage Learning.

Gale and Greenhaven Press are registered trademarks used herein under license.

For more information, contact:
Greenhaven Press
27500 Drake Rd.
Farmington Hills, MI 48331-3535
Or you can visit our Internet site at gale.cengage.com

LIBRARY OF CONGRESS CATALOGING-IN-PUBLICATION DATA

Mixed heritage / Stefan Kiesbye, editor.
    p. cm. -- (Social issues firsthand)
    Includes bibliographical references and index.
    ISBN 978-0-7377-4560-3 (hardcover)
    1. Interracial marriage--United States. 2. Parenting--United States. 3. Group identity--United States. 4. Multiculturalism--United States. I. Kiesbye, Stefan.
    HQ1031.M58 2009
    305.800973--dc22

            2009008628

Printed in the United States of America
1 2 3 4 5 6 7 13 12 11 10 09

Contents

Chapter 1: Growing Up in a Mixed-Heritage Family

Chapter 2: Parenting in Mixed-Heritage Families

Chapter 3: Mixed Heritage in a Multicultural Society

Foreword

Social issues are often viewed in abstract terms. Pressing challenges such as poverty, homelessness, and addiction are viewed as problems to be defined and solved. Politicians, social scientists, and other experts engage in debates about the extent of the problems, their causes, and how best to remedy them. Often overlooked in these discussions is the human dimension of the issue. Behind every policy debate over poverty, homelessness, and substance abuse, for example, are real people struggling to make ends meet, to survive life on the streets, and to overcome addiction to drugs and alcohol. Their stories are ubiquitous and compelling. They are the stories of everyday people—perhaps your own family members or friends—and yet they rarely influence the debates taking place in state capitols, the national Congress, or the courts.

The disparity between the public debate and private experience of social issues is well illustrated by looking at the topic of poverty. Each year the U.S. Census Bureau establishes a poverty threshold. A household with an income below the threshold is defined as poor, while a household with an income above the threshold is considered able to live on a basic subsistence level. For example, in 2003 a family of two was considered poor if its income was less than $12,015; a family of four was defined as poor if its income was less than $18,810. Based on this system, the bureau estimates that 35.9 million Americans (12.5 percent of the population) lived below the poverty line in 2003, including 12.9 million children below the age of eighteen.

Commentators disagree about what these statistics mean. Social activists insist that the huge number of officially poor Americans translates into human suffering. Even many families that have incomes above the threshold, they maintain, are likely to be struggling to get by. Other commentators insist that the statistics exaggerate the problem of poverty in the United States. Compared to people in developing countries, they point out, most so-called poor families have a high quality of life. As stated by journalist Fidelis Iyebote, "Cars are owned by 70 percent of 'poor' households. . . . Color televisions belong to 97 percent of the 'poor' [and] videocassette recorders belong to nearly 75 percent. . . . Sixty-four percent have microwave ovens, half own a stereo system, and over a quarter possess an automatic dishwasher."

However, this debate over the poverty threshold and what it means is likely irrelevant to a person living in poverty. Simply put, poor people do not need the government to tell them whether they are poor. They can see it in the stack of bills they cannot pay. They are aware of it when they are forced to choose between paying rent or buying food for their children. They become painfully conscious of it when they lose their homes and are forced to live in their cars or on the streets. Indeed, the written stories of poor people define the meaning of poverty more vividly than a government bureaucracy could ever hope to. Narratives composed by the poor describe losing jobs due to injury or mental illness, depict horrific tales of childhood abuse and spousal violence, recount the loss of friends and family members. They evoke the slipping away of social supports and government assistance, the descent into substance abuse and addiction, the harsh realities of life on the streets. These are the perspectives on poverty that are too often omitted from discussions over the extent of the problem and how to solve it.

Greenhaven Press's *Social Issues Firsthand* series provides a forum for the often-overlooked human perspectives on society's most divisive topics of debate. Each volume focuses on one social issue and presents a collection of ten to sixteen narratives by those who have had personal involvement with the topic. Extra care has been taken to include a diverse range of perspectives. For example, in the volume on adoption, readers will find the stories of birth parents who have made an adoption plan, adoptive parents, and adoptees themselves. After exposure to these varied points of view, the reader will have a clearer understanding that adoption is an intense, emotional experience full of joyous highs and painful lows for all concerned.

The debate surrounding embryonic stem cell research illustrates the moral and ethical pressure that the public brings to bear on the scientific community. However, while nonexperts often criticize scientists for not considering the potential negative impact of their work, ironically the public's reaction against such discoveries can produce harmful results as well. For example, although the outcry against embryonic stem cell research in the United States has resulted in fewer embryos being destroyed, those with Parkinson's, such as actor Michael J. Fox, have argued that prohibiting the development of new stem cell lines ultimately will prevent a timely cure for the disease that is killing Fox and thousands of others.

Each book in the series contains several features that enhance its usefulness, including an in-depth introduction, an annotated table of contents, bibliographies for further research, a list of organizations to contact, and a thorough index. These elements—combined with the poignant voices of people touched by tragedy and triumph—make the Social Issues Firsthand series a valuable resource for research on today's topics of political discussion.

Introduction

Laura Smith, a British journalist, recounts a first encounter with the challenges that people with mixed heritage face. "When I was three, a little friend of mine pointed at me and said with accusation in her voice: 'You're black.' My response was one that only a three-year-old could make. Puffing up my chest and probably sticking my nose in the air, I told her firmly: 'No, I'm not. I'm pink and brown.' It wasn't that being black was a bad thing. It was just that my skin was not literally the colour of my black crayons and so, logically, what she had said was nonsense."

As innocent as this episode seems, it highlights the difficulty of mixed-heritage persons to give a definition of who they are that does not sound vague or evasive. The very term *mixed heritage* sometimes seems to have sprung from the kitchen—mixed greens, mixed fruit—and a blender comes to mind. College professor Robyn Preston-McGee, who is white, says that whenever "one of my college students who sees [my daughter's] picture in my office asks where she gets her curly hair or if she's 'mixed,' I usually reply, 'Yes, she's biracial' (for I've always thought 'mixed' to be used only for dogs and cocktails)." She adds, "I answer this question three or four times a day and often wonder if I should just stick a sign on her that reads, 'Yes, my father is black.'"

What seems to be missing from language are terms that describe, without discrimination, hate, or contempt, the experience of being biracial or multiracial—especially in a world that still seems to grapple with differences in skin color.

This dilemma becomes apparent in education. Smith writes, "As a group, mixed-race people have persistently underachieved in education. A report commissioned by the Department for Education and Skills in 2004 found that mixed children were ignored by school curricula and by school and local education authority policies on race. The report concluded: 'Their invisibility from policy makes it difficult for their underachievement to be challenged.' The report highlighted a lack of awareness about mixedness among teaching staff and persistent negative stereotyping of mixed-race families."

The lack of awareness is hurtful and permeates much of the everyday life of mixed-race people. The question "What are you?"—not "Who are you?" or "Where do you come from?"—is a constant reminder that in the eyes of our society, mixed-race people do not seem to belong anywhere. Often having difficulty being accepted by any of the communities their parents came from, bi- or multiracial adolescents grow up identifying with no heritage, feeling unmoored. Quoting Clare Felix, national black and minority ethnic (BME) manager for the mental health charity Rethink, Smith writes, "'Mixed people can find it difficult to find cultural affiliations. They might be rejected by their black side because their skin's too light and their hair's too straight, and rejected by their white side because their skin's too dark and their hair's too frizzy.'" Smith echoes this, saying, "There were times as a young person when I wished I was either one or the other. Black, for what I imagined was the privilege of knowing who I was and not feeling somehow diluted, a 'fake black.' White, for the privilege of not having to think about it at all."

Hapa—a Hawaiian term, meaning "half" and originally describing people of mixed Pacific Islander racial/ethnic heritage—has long since been adopted by persons of mixed Asian heritage. It is the rare term that describes a biracial person and also displays a certain pride, providing identification for a wide range of Americans. Though the case has been made that *hapa* was stolen from the Hawaiians, it is nevertheless a rallying term, describing mixed heritage not in a half-hearted and stigmatized manner but in a positive and empowering way. Most Americans with a mixed cultural or racial heritage are missing this type of description.

Part of the conundrum may be that mixed marriages—though on the rise in the United States—are still frowned upon in many communities—white, black, Latino, or Asian. Mixed marriages are often seen as diluting heritage, instead of enriching it. Whether it is to preserve power structures or old customs, or because of long-held prejudice, majorities and minorities can be hostile to people marrying outside their culture or race.

The recent election of Barack Obama, who is biracial, as the U.S. president marks a historical milestone that might be an important step toward the recognition of the unique situation and experience of mixed-race people. Because, apart from the issue of facing rejection, "being mixed does . . . have its advantages," Smith writes. "While I am usually aware of my difference at all-black and all-white gatherings, I have the privilege of being able to fit in with both, and everything in between. My ethnic identity is not fixed, but fluid. My partner, who has a way with words, says it's a bit like being on the fence, able to see into both gardens—black and white—but without a garden of our own. All of us, with our families and friends, have had to create one." Yet even with today's changes, she recognizes that there is still much more work to do. "Now, I see them everywhere. Mixed children being swung in the park between their differently-coloured parents; brown-skinned babies being balanced on the hips of their white mothers; frizzy-haired siblings shopping with their black and white grandmothers. I hope things will be easier for them than they were for me. But in a culture that still sees identity in terms of black, white or Asian, I'm not so sure."

Preston-McGee shares that apprehension, saying, "My white students, for example, joyously remark that 'racism is a thing of the past.' I ask them to consider how their own parents would react if they brought home a black person to marry. A flash of awareness comes across their faces . . . and I already know their answer." It is clear that more change is needed to achieve racial equality and to build those gardens for people of mixed races and ethnicities.

CHAPTER 1

Growing Up in a
Mixed-Heritage Family

Mixed-Heritage Children Need to Transcend Established Communities

Emilie Hammerstein

In this selection, the writer remembers her difficulties finding a group or culture she could call her own. Accepted by neither the Jewish nor the Chinese communities, she sets out to find her very own space and identity within multicultural America but finds that she is unable and finally unwilling to blend in. Emilie Hammerstein graduated from Johns Hopkins University with a BA in English.

"So . . . what are you?" This is a question I can always count on being asked. And this is the answer I automatically respond with: "My mother is Chinese, my father is Jewish. I'm Chinese and Jewish."

Most people first guess that I am Latina, a lucky few ask if I'm part Asian, and so far, I've only heard one person say I look German-Jewish. Two summers ago, before my junior year at Johns Hopkins University in Baltimore, I was waiting for a train when two college-aged guys came up to me: "We don't mean to bother you or anything, but my friend and I wondered if you could settle our argument. He thinks you're Spanish and I think you're Indian. Can you tell us who's right?"

I don't mind people asking me what I am. In some ways, it's flattering: I'm glad that I don't look like everybody else. I'm proud of my heritage—both of my heritages—and I want to share that with the world. However, make no mistakes about it—being mixed is an experience as confusing, messy and emotional as it is beautiful. It is a blessing, but it is equally

Emilie Hammerstein, "Sticky Rice at Yom Kippur," EurasianNation.com, November 2002. Reproduced by permission. http://www.eurasiannation.com/articlesea2002 -11sticky.htm.

a burden. I have often felt that the world is not ready for someone like me, someone who is a walking contradiction to their cultural definitions.

A World of Contradictions

My brother Josh and I grew up in the suburbs of St. Louis, where we had almost no Chinese or Jewish neighbors or classmates, let alone Chinese-Jewish ones. The only time I ever thought about being different was when I was called "Oriental girl" or "Jewish retard" in school. We were the only kids who were excused from class on Rosh Hashanah and Yom Kippur and went home to eat sticky rice and drunken chicken for dinner. But we weren't particularly religious, nor were we well-schooled in Chinese tradition. My mom made me and Josh attend Chinese school on Sundays for a while. My only memories are of snack-time and racing rolling chairs down the halls. The only words I knew growing up were pigoo (ass), lien (face), and tang-tang (candy). And to be honest, the only reason I knew pigoo and lien was so that Josh and I could call each other "butt-face" in Chinese.

When I was eleven, our family moved to Pittsburgh and I started attending a very small, private all-girls school. Out of my class of 40 girls, about one-fourth of them were Jewish. It was a shock to me to suddenly realize that I wasn't like them at all. In St. Louis, being the only Jewish girl in school was what made me different and set me apart from everyone else. That was how I identified myself. In Pittsburgh, I found out that my unusual upbringing put me at odds with my Jewish classmates. I didn't go to Hebrew school and my parents weren't planning an elaborate bat mitzvah for me. Another mixed girl in my class (she was half black, half white) hissed at me, "You're not Jewish, you're only half-Jewish." Technically, though, there is no such thing as half-Jewish. Judaism is passed on through matrilineal descent. If your mother is Jewish and your father is not, you're still considered Jewish. However, if you have a Jewish father and a non-Jewish mother, then you are not considered Jewish. When my mom married my dad, she converted to Judaism under the Reform movement, which is the least stringent faction of the religion. I was brought up as a Reform Jew. I am not considered Jewish by many people. They do not regard how I was brought up to be a factor in my identity. Nor what religion I identify with most. Nor what my family died for in the concentration camps.

No Place to Fit In

It didn't help that my mother had become a born-again Christian around the time I was twelve. Our home had never been particularly peaceful, but by the time I reached adolescence, my mom and I were waging a full-fledged religious war. I was uncomfortable with her new practices. The real problem, however, was that she wanted me and Josh to renounce Judaism entirely and convert. When we refused, she made a deal with my father: she would stop attending church if we stopped going to the synagogue. My father agreed, but in the end, she didn't hold up her end of the deal.

From high school on, I harbored uneasy feelings that I did not belong. I started studying Hebrew in my spare time in order to feel more connected to my background and, perhaps subconsciously, to seem more Jewish to others. During my senior year of high school, my classmates and I were asked to split up into groups, according to our ethnicity for a group exercise. I asked the teacher, "What if you have two ethnicities?" "Just pick one," she answered. Inwardly, I was upset and confused. It wasn't simply the exercise. I felt that I was constantly forced to choose between my two backgrounds without actually belonging to either.

By the time I entered college at Hopkins, I felt something was missing. I wanted to belong to a community, a group that understood where I came from. So, I became active in the Jewish Students' Association. I was self-conscious about being mixed and would avoid talking about my mother's background whenever possible. Eventually, though, I was known as the "Asian-Jewish girl." Then I was told by several members of the ultra-Orthodox community (and on several separate occasions) that I wasn't really Jewish and in order to be accepted, I would have to undergo an Orthodox conversion—no simple feat. In the words of a Chabad (ultra-orthodox Jew) who ran a Jewish education program at Hopkins, the Jewish community was an "extended family" and I was "not a member" of the family unless I converted. I was utterly and completely degraded.

Feeling Bitter

I felt both ashamed of myself and angry at those who judged me for something I could not control: Why did I have to be born mixed? Why couldn't I just be one or the other, a simple either/or? I never looked Chinese enough to fit in with the Asian crowd and I lacked a traditional upbringing that would make me feel at home among the Jewish community. If I sound a little bitter, it's because I am. You would think that college students would be mature enough to have outgrown racial stereotyping, especially at a campus as diverse as Johns Hopkins, whose reputation in medicine attracts a large percentage of international students and roughly 20% of students on campus are Asian. Unfortunately, I learned that this is not so. To a certain sector of Jewish students on campus, I was known as "Chopsticks" behind my back. One Shabbat dinner, I happened to mention that most people don't think I look Chinese. To this, I was answered, "Yes, you do. You have slanty eyes."

My cousin Alice, jokes that Jews are often attracted to Chinese, especially Chinese women. When I tell people that I don't have any cousins who aren't at least half-Chinese, including on my father's side, I typically hear a response that I have come to loathe, "Ooh, your family's got an Asian fetish, huh?" People imagine the Asian wife as uneducated, subservient and exotic. They ask how my parents met, usually assuming that my father served in the armed services abroad, met my mother in a small rural village and married her. In reality, my mother is from Taipei, a city known for being modern, educated and cosmopolitan. She was the first member of her family to move to the United States after receiving a B.A. in English from University of Taipei. She didn't marry my father for a green card either. My parents met because they were both working for Time Life Books in Manhattan.

Even with my own relatives, I felt vaguely out-of-place. One time, my mom was talking to a Chinese cook as I stood by her side. When she mentioned I was her daughter, the chef replied, "Ah! Wo xiang ta shi waiguoren." I thought she was a foreigner. The word *waiguoren* is usually used to refer to anyone who is not Chinese. Literally, it means "outsider." I do feel like an outsider, even in my own family. No one would assume that I'm my mother's daughter; some people have assumed that I'm my father's wife. My brother and I don't look like anyone in our family besides each other. It hurts a little to look at pictures of my grandparents, searching for traces of myself and finding none.

Excluded from Claiming a Heritage

Furthermore, my parents don't understand why I feel rejected by traditional Asian and Jewish communities. They can't relate to my feelings about being mixed nor to the sense of confusion that stems from it. They don't understand that it can be confusing for me to constantly be asked, "What are you?" I never had to think about what I was until other people wanted to know how to define me. And, unlike generations of my family before me, I'm not always sure what I am. Sometimes, I feel more connected to one heritage than the other and vice versa. My parents' well-intentioned but overly-simplified logic is this: they are Chinese and Jewish and I am their daughter

... therefore, the world must see me as a reflection of themselves, that is, Chinese or Jewish. They don't understand that my filial connection to them isn't so evident to everyone else and it's not so easy to explain being Chinese and Jewish. My mom has said to me, "Your brother doesn't feel this way, he doesn't have problems with being mixed." It's true that not all mixed kids are confused about their cultural and societal identity, but every Hapa [mixed Asian and/or Hawaiian heritage] experience is distinct, just like every Hapa is unique.

Hapas have to face a slew of issues that no other ethnic group has had to face before. The age we live in is unique because, although we are not the first of our kind, our generation is the result of an unprecedented number of mixed marriages. The issue of space becomes important. One must find one's own space in society, in the world. Communities are traditionally formed to bind a type of people together within a space. But mixed children are faced with the task of transcending established communities in pursuit of their own space in the world. Because I feel uncomfortable in both Chinese and Jewish communities, I must create a unique niche for myself.

A New Melting Pot

Paradoxically, being mixed is simultaneously anti-American and the purest definition of what it means to be American. Ideally, the United States was established as a melting pot—a land where people of all races and ethnicities could live and multiply together and, ultimately, become one people. In some ways, though, America is still more of a tossed salad than a true melting pot. The phenomenon of the hyphenated American is undeniable within our society. It remains important for families to preserve the same customs and way of life as their ancestors. And yet, at the same time, the number of mixed children is growing rapidly; on the Johns Hopkins campus alone, there were a large number of Amerasians, resulting in a student group called Hapa. The truth is that at this point in time, mixed kids straddle two worlds. We are caught between a society that still forces us to define ourselves by some kind of hyphenated American label and a world whose face is being changed forever by technology and the globalization of trade and travel.

From my own experiences, I now have mixed feelings about intermarriages and mixed relationships. While on the one hand, I believe that race or religion shouldn't be a deciding factor in love, I do feel that it is important to perpetuate traditions through your children. However, I have no choice—my marriage will be a mixed marriage, no matter whom I marry. Unless, that is, I happen to marry another Chinese Jew, which I find unlikely. This leaves me wondering: what will I pass on to my children? Part of the joy of having children is the knowledge that you can instill in them the same beliefs and cultural values that your parents passed on to you. One of my greatest fears is that in future generations, my own culture and influence will only dwindle.

Seeking to Be Understood

At this point in my life, I feel more inclined to date Hapa men than anyone else. This decision is not simply a result of my desire to pass traditions I grew up with on to my children. I would be lying if I said that weren't a factor; however, much stronger than that is my desire to be with someone who understands me to the very core. Being mixed has shaped who I am. It may seem ironic that even though I have the freedom to date or marry whomever I want (after all, I am the product of an interracial marriage), I would choose to be with a Hapa. Some could see my preference as a perpetuation of traditional, monoracial dating standards. But just because we're Hapas, does that mean we have an obligation to date outside of our race? In reality, my decision is really a personal choice to be with someone who can relate to me. After all, I would never restrict myself to dating only mixed men since I know first-hand how much it can hurt to be judged solely on the basis of ethnicity. Besides, with this freedom, is it really surprising that I would decide to be with someone like me?

Now, when people ask me, "What are you?" I consciously refrain from saying that I'm half-Chinese and half-Jewish. I am Chinese and Jewish. I'm not half and half, I am whole. I am an individual. It no longer bothers me to mark my ethnicity as "Other" on forms. It's taken me a while to accept who I am and be proud of it. I'm not a mutt, I am a "strong, healthy mix" as a cousin and her husband, both doctors, put it. Why not take pride in being a Hapa, a mixed-blood child, a Eurasian, an Amerasian? After all, mixed kids are physically healthier and many people assert that we're smarter and better-looking, too. As we enter the 21st century, you see more and more of us in the public eye. Actors Jennifer Tilly and Dean Cain, gold-medal speed skater Apolo Anton Ohno and supermodel Devon Aoki all share the strange, unique, wonderful experience with us. It's hard to understand what it means, unless you experience it yourself.

Leaving a Multitude of Cultures

I realize that ultimately, being mixed has made me a better person with a rich cultural background. I've worked hard to compensate for the conventional Chinese and Jewish upbringing I never had by exploring my roots. For a while, I immersed myself in Jewish tradition, culture and education. My lack of tradition growing up incited me to learn as much as I did. In the end, however, I realized that I would never fully belong to that community, not just because of the way my mother converted or my "slanty" eyes, but because I was raised differently and exposed to various cultures and communities. In the same spirit, I studied Chinese for several years at Hopkins. My initial embarrassment at my poor accent and slow learning eventually evolved into a genuine love for the language and culture. I was thrilled when I realized that I could finally understand my family's conversations. Best of all, for the first time in my life, I could communicate with my grandparents myself and not through my mother or a relative. And they appreciated it. My Chinese is rusty, but to my grandparents, it's perfect. Learning it was my way of saying how much I loved and valued them—they didn't need a translator to tell them that much.

Now, I live my life according to the principles my parents instilled in me and I celebrate what is important to me—Chinese and Jewish alike. The way in which we are raised has the greatest impact on our identities—it shapes what we need, what we want and who we are. I can at last accept that my identity is a mixture of ideals and traditions. Almost six months ago, I watched my beautiful, beloved grandmother lie on her deathbed, finally succumbing to the cancer she fought for ten years. The last time she was lucid enough to recognize me, she gasped out words that she had told me all my life. I never understood what she was saying until a few years ago. "Ni . . . tinghua." Listen. Listen to what your parents say. When I was younger, those words made me feel unworthy, but now I finally understand what she was saying. I know that I inhabit two different worlds and I am the possessor of two cultures. I am my parents' daughter and they have passed their culture and heritage down to me. I must define myself by what I know and not by what others think of me.

Growing Up in an Interfaith Family Strengthens Tolerance

Samie Facciolo

Practicing Judaism, her mother's religion, the author grows up also being exposed to Catholicism, her father's faith. Out of her mixed-heritage experience grows her understanding and acceptance of cultural and religious experience. Samie Facciolo attended the American University in Washington, D.C.

While I was growing up in an interfaith family, I practiced only Judaism with my mother while my younger brother and my father practiced only Catholicism. That division was my parents' decision. When I was born, they agreed to raise me in the Jewish tradition, and when my brother was born, they agreed to raise him in the Catholic tradition. As I grew a bit older, I began to appreciate the religious plurality and respect that grew out of my upbringing. Around age nine, I remember declaring to my father my intention to only marry someone who was non-Jewish so my children could experience the same religious acceptance that pervaded my childhood. Since then, my perspectives and ideas have changed, but my intentions of cultivating a home full of religious understanding have not.

Growing up, I faced daily choices concerning my religious perspectives as well as the constant challenge of practicing my faith while maintaining respect for the faiths of others. I had to decide how to grow in my Jewish faith while appreciating my brother's parallel growth in Catholicism, and how to explore my father's Catholicism from an intellectual standpoint while maintaining Jewish practices and beliefs. I realized that sitting with my father at Easter morning Mass would not diminish my Judaism and later that I could maintain Jewish beliefs while attending a Catholic high school that, despite the difficulties its religious atmosphere would present, offered me the academic challenge and college preparation I sought. I learned how to celebrate Catholic holidays with my father's family in a way that was comfortable for me but that did not detract from the religious significance those holidays held for them. However, one choice I never felt compelled to make was whether I wanted to be Catholic or not. For me, Judaism has always been a sanctuary. It has always been an arena where I have felt comfortable pursuing faith and spiritual growth. As a little girl, I respected the religious fulfillment my father and his mother found when they entered a church, but I sought my faith in a Jewish setting.

Disagreement Led to Tolerance

When I came home from Hebrew school and my brother came home from CRE (Catholic Religious Education) classes, we would compare textbooks, and our comparisons would inevitably lead to a discussion of the values contained within the texts and our confusion over the different views on specific issues. I remember being puzzled that someone growing up with me could learn such contrasting views on certain topics. Whereas by his bedside table my little brother would line up miniature statues of St. Anthony and St. Joseph, I disagreed with the concept that saints could act as intermediaries between God and people's prayers. He learned that saints and priests served to intercept and deliver prayers to God, while I learned that prayer was a direct connection to God. We had grandmothers who taught us both how to make charoset (a Passover dish usually made with apples, nuts and wine) and to say blessings over candles on the one side, and how to say the Our Father prayer and to use holy water from

France on the other side, but we each had a parent instilling in us the beliefs of our own religion.

Even as a little girl, I recognized the difference in attitudes that existed between most of my friends and me. They grew up in households strictly of one religion and felt free to enthusiastically embrace their religions without having a brother learning catechism and practicing for his First Communion alongside them. While I had the freedom to embrace Judaism, my interfaith family always reminded me that other people delve into their religions with just as much conviction and eagerness. Therefore, my earliest experiences in Judaism were also my first experiences in an interfaith setting, and respect for other religions grew parallel to my knowledge of Hebrew letters and synagogue prayers.

I spent this past fall in Santiago, Chile, and during that time I lived with an Orthodox Jewish family. While I experienced differences in our living styles, I felt privileged to have the opportunity to witness this family's interactions and the effects their Jewish practices had on their lives. In this family, we ate Shabbat (Sabbath) dinner together every Friday night and shared Shabbat and other holiday meals with the small Orthodox community of Santiago. Religious articles filled their home, and my host parents took pride in sharing rituals. They supported each other in their religious practices and built a warm family environment of Jewish practice and belief.

Looking for Community

As I moved through college and into the wider Jewish community of synagogue, Jewish organizations on campus and Jewish academic, volunteer and social groups, I realized that many of the characteristics present during my home stay in Chile are elements I would like to incorporate into my future home. Linking my family to the wider Jewish community and having the freedom to celebrate Jewish events within the supportive context of relationships with a spouse and children are ideas I did not consider as a child. I have begun to weigh these ideals alongside the concept of an interfaith family that I held so strongly earlier in life.

As an adult, I realize that I could cultivate acceptance of other religions in a Jewish household just as I could build Jewish values in an interfaith home. At this point in my life, I would be happy to marry someone who is Jewish and to raise my children with open-minded Jewish values and practices. My mother raised me to treasure Jewish traditions and precepts as my own, while respecting my father's Catholic beliefs and rituals. At the same time, she gave me an understanding of *why* I should hold such respect for other people's faiths. I am confident that I could instill the same values and ideas in my own children without necessarily needing to live in an interfaith home.

In the past, my interfaith family guided me to cultivate an open mind toward others' religions and an understanding of their faiths, and in the future I hope these experiences will lead me toward shaping a Jewish home with the same ideals.

Being Raised Jewish and Irish

William S. Cohen

In the following selection from his memoirs, William S. Cohen recalls the difficulties of fitting in as the son of an Irish Catholic mother and a Jewish father. Regarded with suspicion by some in the Jewish community, he also has had to fend off anti-Semitism. Cohen is a former U.S. secretary of defense, U.S. senator, and U.S. congressman.

It was my father, Reuben Cohen, who insisted that I have the benefit of a Jewish education. It was a reasonable enough request to the firstborn son of a Jewish baker. Even my mother, Clara Hartley, thought it was a good idea.

Wait. Clara Hartley? Sounds Irish.

Indeed.

And that really was my beginning.

They had met at a dance hall in 1937 at a place called the Auto Rest Park, located just a few miles outside of Bangor's city limits. Clara Irene Hartley was just sixteen. Her mother had died when she was a young child and she was raised by a father who had a touch of wanderlust. He moved her, her sister, Lena, and brother, Donald, from small town to small town in rural northern Maine before finally locating in Bangor.

She was five feet five inches in height, but stood so erect that she seemed a half a foot taller. Blond, blue-eyed, and stunningly beautiful (my father would always recount how her cheeks were the color of apple skins), she captured his heart immediately. Within weeks after my father met her, they were married. She obviously didn't marry him for his money. At the time, he was making a grand total of six dollars a week at

William S. Cohen with Janet Langhart Cohen, *Love in Black and White: A Memoir of Race, Religion, and Romance,* Lanham, MD: Rowman & Littlefield, 2007. Copyright © 2007 by William S. Cohen. All rights reserved. Reproduced by permission.

the bakery. While they were not poor, there were few material conveniences they could afford to purchase. I can still recall my mother washing our clothes on a scrub board in a cast-iron bathtub. A modest level of prosperity did not enter our lives until the war ended.

Interfaith Marriage Was Frowned Upon

Their marriage was kept a secret from his father, Harry Cohen, for months. When he learned that my mother was pregnant with my sister, Marlene, he did not greet the news of his impending grandfather status with great enthusiasm. My father had crossed a bright red line that divided Jew from Gentile. The mixing of bloodlines was a great taboo, and he had broken it. There were consequences to follow his transgression, but at the time, love had overwhelmed all fear.

There's little doubt in my mind that my father was trying to please Granpa by showing him that his son would carry on the revered Jewish tradition.

I was only five years old at the time, and it was not clear to me exactly what "Jewish" meant at the time, but I was to find out that it meant that I was not "Catholic."

One day, two of my neighborhood friends, Karl and Paul, pleaded with me to accompany them to St. John's Catholic Church. They explained to me that in addition to the pews inside the church where you could kneel to pray, there were confessional booths where you could unburden your soul. First, I wasn't convinced that I had ever sinned. Sure, I had dispensed a few choice expletives while jousting in the streets. And, yes, I had occasionally stepped on a crack in the pavement and had "broken my mother's back," according to the superstition then in vogue. But that hardly condemned me to a one-way ticket to damnation. Moreover the very thought of whispering to a man called "Father," who was not my father, that I had indulged in sinful conduct was out of the question.

After assuring me that I could skip the confessional booth, my pals finally persuaded me to venture into the cavernous interior of the church—just to watch.

Visiting a Church

Upon entering the church, I saw the vaulted ceilings and the worshippers kneeling in prayer and felt immediately uncomfortable. The atmosphere was totally alien to anything I had experienced. The church was dark, mystical, intimidating. I followed my friends to a pew and tried not to look out of place. When I saw Paul and Karl drop down on their knees, I followed suit with some hesitation. The act of kneeling was baffling to me, simply because I had never observed anyone doing it at the Jewish synagogue.

I was confused and embarrassed, much as I had been in my first grade classroom in the Abraham Lincoln Elementary School. I had always refused to pray in public school, and when my teacher and the other students asked why, I explained that I was Jewish and we recited different prayers. I would later discover that my answer was only half true. In any event, the answer seemed satisfactory to everyone but me, because I still didn't understand the harm in reciting the Twenty-third Psalm in the Bible.

There were, in fact, many things that I didn't understand. I had started to learn simplified versions of the Old Testament. I could not comprehend how God could erupt with such emotion whenever someone displeased him. Sending forth locusts, frogs, famine, and other forms of ingenious punishment seemed, well, unGod-like. Moses, after spending forty years in the desert, strikes a rock in a moment of frustration, and he gets to see the Promised Land from a mountaintop! And precisely why was it that we could never spell the word God but had to omit the letter "o"? Was it really irreverent to spell the full name of our Creator? If so, why were we allowed to say the word itself? Was it sacrilegious for me to have these doubts or express these thoughts? What were the penalties for doing so?

Religious Doubts

At the end of the service I watched as people proceeded, single file, toward the front of the church, where a priest awaited them. I hesitated at first. The priest had a somber mien about him that struck me as uninviting and unfriendly. Surely he knew that I was not a young Catholic boy! The idea of participating in this activity absolutely terrified me. "I'll stay here," I whispered. Paul and Karl wouldn't hear of it. "Come on, Billy," they whispered. I protested further but stopped short of creating a disturbance. Playground pressure won out and I followed them to the altar. I completed my visit to St. John's with a consecrated wafer and a smudge of ash on my forehead.

While walking home I had no idea that I'd just celebrated the first day of Lent and that now I was supposed to go through the next forty weekdays until Easter in a period of fasting and penitence. I felt no guilt or shame for my entry into forbidden territory, that is, not until later that evening, when my grandfather spotted me with the identifiable smudge on my forehead. That bit of ash I was sporting caused my grandfather to turn menacing toward me for the very first time. Out of his anger came one demand after another.

"Where have you been? What have you done? We're Jewish," he scolded me. "Don't go to St. John's ever again."

This was how I learned that being Jewish excluded any notion that I might also be Catholic. No one at the time thought it necessary to explain to me the fundamental tenets of each religion. I was left dangling in a dark void to ponder the significance of my transgression. My grandfather was content to strike my heart with fear. His reprimand worked. Until I reached adulthood, I never stepped inside another church.

Religious Instruction

By the time I was seven, I was ready to begin in earnest the process that would instruct me in detail about what it meant to be Jewish. In Hebrew school there would be meaning attached to the customs and traditions that separated me from my peers. Unfortunately, my experience at Hebrew school, which I attended three times per week after public school, proved to be more exasperating than anything I had anticipated.

From the very beginning of my religious instruction, I felt like the proverbial odd man out. I had friends who attended both of the schools with me, so it was not a question of my being surrounded by strangers. The problem lay in my lineage. My mother's genes had proved dominant over my father's. I was constantly reminded that my face was the very map of Ireland. My blond hair stood in stark contrast to the darker Semitic look of nearly everyone else.

I felt most self-conscious about my appearance during the High Holidays. I was five when I first started going to the Beth Abraham Synagogue with my father. There were three synagogues in Bangor at the time, all located in the same area as St. Johns Catholic Church: Beth Abraham, Beth Israel, and Toldoth and Yitzchak. The three synagogues represented the Conservative, Reform, and Orthodox philosophies. I never understood the distinction except that Beth Israel was more elegant in design, with its stone and cement-block construction, ornate columns, and domed superstructure. It made the two other nearby wooden-framed buildings look like poor second cousins. The men and women who worshipped at Beth Israel were noticeably different in appearance. Their dress, manner, and confidence seemed, well, superior. In fact, it was a class distinction that separated Beth Israel from the others. Its members traced their lineage to German and Baltic states rather than to Poland or Russia. They were mostly professionals—doctors, lawyers, accountants, entrepreneurs. Their counterparts at the other synagogues consisted of the butchers, bakers, and candlestick makers—small shop owners, peddlers, and junk dealers, men whose hands bore the calluses of manual work, lower-middle-class people who had not yet crossed the lines that marked the gentile neighborhoods.

It was only during Rosh Hashanah and Yom Kippur that my father closed the bakery. While the orthodox members would walk to the synagogue, my father placed a higher premium on convenience. Surely, he would not disturb the universe by driving his automobile during the High Holidays. His only concession to convention was to park the family car several blocks away from the synagogue and then walk the remaining distance so as to not make a flagrant display of his disregard for tradition.

Alienation

From my very earliest moments in the synagogue, the strongest emotion I experienced was a sense of alienation. The men who attended the services were mostly dark complected. They dressed in dark suits, complemented with dark, broad-brimmed hats. Their hats were replaced with yarmulkes and silk "tallises" (shawls) as they entered the synagogue. Once seated, many of the men would take a pinch of snuff (aromatic tobacco) from small boxes, make a fist, place the snuff in the area formed by the thumb and forefinger, and then inhale it. (Many years later I would witness German chancellor Helmut Schmidt do precisely the same thing during a private meeting in his office.) Some of them would wrap tefillin (black straps containing prayer boxes) tightly around their arms in preparation for prayer.

I had apparel of my own, of course. I had a tallis and yarmulke that I kept in a soft maroon-colored felt bag with the Star of David embroidered on it in gold thread. But while clothes make—or conceal—the man, these religious accoutrements could not transform me into something I clearly was not.

Beth Abraham was a modest building that accommodated a series of benches on one level and a balcony above. I was particularly struck by the fact that in the synagogue men and women were not allowed to mix together in the pews. The women were all seated upstairs. It struck me as odd, but my father had a unique opinion, which he shared with me. "You don't want the women seated with the men," he explained. "Women are a distraction, see?"

I learned later that under Jewish law, women were considered to be "unclean," and were forbidden to be seated in close proximity to the men. It was in retrospect a form of "separate but equal" segregation, albeit one that I suspected lasted only during the religious ceremonies of the day.

Confusing Rituals

In contrapuntal response to the presiding cantor, the men would recite passages from prayer books while standing and "dovening" (bending slightly and rhythmically) at the waist. Up in the balcony, women were wailing in grief over the loss of their loved ones. I found the sound of the ram's horn (shofar) that was being blown amusing, but inexplicable. In fact I thought the ceremonies were just as strange and incomprehensible as anything I had witnessed at St. John's Catholic Church on Ash Wednesday.

During the course of the day, there would be periodic breaks from the service and the men would gather on the street outside and engage in animated discussions. I would stay close to my father's side while he either joked with the others or offered his opinions on politics, business, a neighbor's health, or the state of international affairs. He seemed to relish the interaction, slipping periodically into Yiddish, oblivious to my discomfort.

The fact that I clung to my father and that I could recite a few words of the Jewish prayers was insufficient to acquire a stamp—or even a glance—of approval. Occasionally, a comment would be directed my way. "Who's that little goyim?" someone would ask. "That's Ruby Cohen's son. Ruby's married to the Irish broad that won't talk to anyone."

Part of the problem that I faced was that my father was not able to communicate to me a strong belief in the Jewish religion. It was obvious to me that he attended the services out of a sense of duty rather than belief. He was firmly committed to the moral code contained in the Ten Commandments, but found the rituals of religion to be of little appeal. No student of theology, he was a model of inconsistency.

Inconsistent Teaching

During an evening at the dinner table he would say, "No, Billy, I just don't buy any of the nonsense that organized religion pumps out. When it's over, it's over. Just like when you turn the lights out, it just goes dark. Leading a good life is its own reward." A few days later, without conceding any contradiction, he would suggest that a higher, albeit indefinable, intelligence had to have constructed the miraculous chain of life. "I mean, how else can you explain it? Everything in existence serves a higher purpose. It couldn't have happened by accident. Someone or something had to have created it."

I concluded that he was a cautious agnostic: not sure that an Old or New Testament God existed, but unwilling to take any chances that one did not.

My mother rarely engaged in any disputations. She shared my father's disdain for the ceremonious aspects of religion, but held to a simple faith in the existence of an afterlife, the location of which was determined by one's thoughts and actions while alive.

The only explanation for my father's insisting that I attend Hebrew school to study the history, language, and customs of his forebears was that he was convinced that most Jews lived by a superior code of conduct that helped carry them into the higher realms of professional excellence and was an association that I would benefit from. I suspected that deep down he wanted to persuade his peers that he had, after all, produced a nice Jewish boy.

I spent the next six years attempting to prove my commitment to the Jewish faith. While I was an excellent student, things did not go well for me in Hebrew school. Rabbi Saul Brown, a man who was conservative in appearance and manner, had a problem with me. Frequently, he would seek to embarrass me in front of the other students by insisting on a show of hands as to whether our parents kept a kosher house. Predictably, my hand would not be among those that shot up. He publicly upbraided me one day after he had driven by our house and seen a Christmas tree in the window. My mother had joked to me that it was just a Chanukah bush, but Rabbi Brown was not amused.

Between Two Worlds

Knowing of Rabbi Brown's dislike for me only intensified my desire to achieve the highest academic grades each year. My goal was to win the top prize of attending Camp Lown during the summer months. I knew that my parents could not afford the incidental costs associated with the camp, but I wanted the recognition for my achievement anyway. Instead of the invitation to enjoy a summer at the camp, I received a gold-plated mezuzah that contained a small piece of parchment inside with words taken from [the book of] Deuteronomy. At first, I thought it was an oversight. On the second occasion, I recognized it as outright rejection. It was unacceptable to Rabbi Saul and the school's directors that the best student was not a real Jew.

I was suspended between two worlds. Every day at public school I proclaimed myself to be Jewish, refusing to recite the

Lord's Prayer. Yet in Hebrew school I was treated as a non-Jew. I sought refuge from the confusion and an outlet for my anger by joining the YMCA. Yes, the Young Men's Christian Association.

Ever since the days when I sat on my father's lap watching high school basketball games, I dreamed of the time when I would exhibit my skills before thousands of fans. I asked my father permission to attend practice one Saturday each month with the promise that I would attend religious services on the other three weekends. I knew that his love for basketball would overcome any doubts he had about my absence from the synagogue. But my passion for the sport intensified with each incident of rejection at Hebrew school.

Soon I was playing organized basketball two Saturdays a month, then three. While I continued to excel in my Hebrew school studies, I eventually stopped attending Saturday services entirely. This created a problem for me at Hebrew school because the teachers insisted that all students attend Saturday services. Records were kept as to which classes maintained the best attendance. Classes with the best attendance were awarded gold stars and prizes at the end of the year. My absences bred a good deal of resentment. Occasionally, the resentment would erupt into scuffles in the playground area outside the school. Because I was bigger and eager to fight, the scuffles didn't last very long. I knew it was selfish of me to choose basketball over my classmates' aspirations, but because I knew that I was not considered one of them, I was not going to let them force me to accept either their rules or their goals.

A Big Surprise

Pride is said to go before the fall, but I was completely surprised to learn what Rabbi Brown had in store for me as I approached my thirteenth birthday and the prize of being bar mitzvahed. I was about to commence my studies for the upcoming ceremony. I had already practiced my ability to read

Hebrew and committed prayers to memory, but the studying process itself would take several months of intensive training with my rabbi. Before my studies commenced, however, Rabbi Brown called me into his office after class one evening and explained that there were certain preconditions I had to fulfill before he could prepare me for my official entry into manhood. A quiet foreboding, cool as fog, began to roll up the back of my neck.

"You see, Zev," he began, his accent thickening with each word, "there's a ceremony that must be performed before you can be bar mitzvahed."

"What kind of ceremony?" I asked suspiciously.

"Your mother is not Jewish."

"So?"

"Either your mother must convert to Judaism—"

He paused, knowing the impossibility of such a prospect. My mother had never once displayed any interest in becoming a member of any church, religious organization, or community. She professed a simple faith in God and a profound disaffection for any attempt to pressure her into social conformity. While she never voiced any opposition to my attending Hebrew school, she refused to give any consideration to entering a synagogue with my father. She was Irish, a proud, if not practicing, Christian who had no intention of engaging in a theological conversion.

"Or what?" I pushed to have my reluctant mentor spell out my options, layering a certain pugnacity to my voice as a sign that I knew that the goalposts were about to be moved for me once again.

"Then you must undergo a conversion ceremony."

"Which consists of what?" It was not really a question, but rather a demand that he spell out exactly what further concessions I'd have to make. His answer exceeded the bounds of my worst suspicions.

I would have to be submerged in a pool of holy water. Whether it ran from the tap of Rabbi Brown's home or was to be imported from the Sea of Galilee remained unclear, but holy it would be. My submersion would be witnessed and presided over by a small group of Jewish community elders. Now the thought of undergoing a baptismal dunking of sorts was not particularly intimidating. After all, I had spent the last five years leaping naked into the chlorine-laced waters at the YMCA under the watchful eyes of its adult employees. There, of course, I was among peers and I was not seeking acceptance or approval, only perfecting the art of survival.

Rebellion

Had the ceremony consisted only of this one symbolic act, I would have accepted it. But there was more. It seemed that from me more would always be demanded, in endlessly creative ways, to compensate for having a gentile's blood in my veins. A drop of that blood, Rabbi Brown informed me, would have to be extracted from my penis.

I was dumbstruck, first with horror, then with undiluted anger. Why hadn't this been explained to me in the very beginning? Why did I have to endure six years of instruction, of perfecting my ability to read Hebrew, of receiving mezuzahs and medallions, of being chided for living in a nonkosher home, of . . .?

I managed to trap a stream of expletives behind tightly clenched jaws. I turned away from Rabbi Brown and walked, slowly at first, then burst through the door and ran down the stairs and out into the street. I ran without stopping for nearly two miles until I reached home.

Out of breath and choking back tears, I shouted, "I'm not going to do it. I'm not going to do it."

When my father came home that evening, I explained to him what had happened at school and repeated that I wouldn't agree to participate in any conversion ceremony.

"You don't have to, Billy," he said with a profound sadness. He had been looking forward to witnessing his eldest son's proficiency with the words and ways of his Jewish forebears, but at that moment, after seeing the anger in my mother's eyes, he knew that the dream had vanished. To this day, whatever measure of independence I display, I owe almost exclusively to her rock-solid pride and resolve.

My father's disappointment quickly evolved into resentment over the retroactive application of rules that had never been made clear to him. "They wouldn't act this way down in Boston," he fumed. "I could take you down to Dorchester and get you a bar mitzvah with no questions asked!"

For the very first time, I sensed that he finally understood the acts of discrimination I had been experiencing all along. He was so upset over the treatment I had received that he never returned to the synagogue again.

I Am Made Up
of Contradictions

Jon Lewis-Katz

Having a Caribbean mother and a white father, the author grows up feeling rejected by both the black and white communities. He realizes that there is no culture or community that he fits into entirely; rather, he will be an outsider all his life.

One spring afternoon, I stood on the curb and watched my older cousin, who is actually my mother's cousin's son, hail a cab. Or, I should say, try to. For some reason, regardless of whether it held passengers, no taxi stopped for him.

With each failed attempt, I took a step toward the street. Soon, I was in front of him, my right arm extended into 6th Avenue traffic. The first cab at which I motioned stopped.

Inside, my cousin, who is black, explained how he gets cabs where he lives, in our nation's capital. Though he dresses well, in clothes that fit him and have the names of well-known white designers on the labels, cab drivers rarely stop for him. Occasionally, one will and when that happens, he adds the driver's name and number to a list. On Friday afternoons, he dials the cabbies on the list hoping that one of them is on duty that night. If not, he stays in rather than drive drunk.

All this just to catch a cab, I thought as we passed Madison Square Garden. All this, that, because I'm light skinned, I've never had to deal with.

Growing Up in a White Neighborhood

I grew up in Pacific Palisades, where I was one-half of the one and a half black kids in my neighborhood. There were, of course, others. Three, maybe four more of us, besides the kids

Jon Lewis-Katz, "'Is That Your Kid?'" *Pasadena Weekly*, March 9, 2006. Reproduced by permission. http://www.pasadenaweekly.com/cms/story/detail/?id=3171&IssueNum=10.

who rode in on LAUSD [Los Angeles Unified School District] buses. But it felt like we were the only ones. In a way, Sean and I were privileged. We were the only two kids in our Episcopalian school allowed to use the N-word. We were the only ones who had the right to wear baggy clothes. The only ones with a claim to rap music. In short, we were the two admitted to the VIP room of racial stereotypes.

Nevertheless, outside the tiny universe populated by my mostly white schoolmates and their parents, I was reminded that my mom's skin was much darker than mine. I frequently accompanied her on shopping excursions that took us out of the neighborhood, to places filled with people who looked more like my mom than I did. It was then—shopping for clothes, bikes, groceries—that I heard my mom repeatedly asked the same question: "Is that your kid?" Even in our community, at my sports games, people would commonly mistake my mom for my nanny.

As a young child, the idea of race was never explained to me the way reproduction or the multiplication tables were. I think this was my parents' attempt to shelter me. Still, though I lacked racial terminology, I was aware of skin color from a very young age. "Why don't I look like you?" I asked my mom after examining my eyes or lips or nose in the mirror. I don't remember what she said but I recall that it was inadequate. How can you explain to a young child the crapshoot of genetics?

My mom never appeared bothered by the questions people asked. Yes, he's my son, she'd say. Or, no, I'm not my son's nanny.

She was also struggling with racial issues of her own.

Race Matters

She came to this country from the Caribbean at the age of 18 and, more than 40 years later, continues to resist how Americans define race. When I called her African American, she said, "I'm West Indian," meaning that she's from the Caribbean. When I asked why blacks nodded to her on the street, she said, "It's something blacks in this country do."

My mom, though she's brown skinned, has a foreign accent and is usually accepted by whites and blacks. I, on the other hand, found I was an outsider with strangers from both groups. Blacks often openly discriminated against me while whites unknowingly pushed me away by making subtly racist comments (I can't count the times I've heard the phrase, "Big black guy").

Probably because she rejected American racial values, my mom always reminded me that I was not black nor white but mixed. My mom's line, however, either met ridicule (I once asked a light-skinned African American kid what flavor Gatorade he was drinking. "Citrus," he said. "Like you.") or was deemed insufficient ("So then, what are you?" they asked, repeating the question I'd thought I just answered. "My mom's black, my dad's white," I said).

As I grew, my skin tone didn't change and even though my nose grew a little wider, my lips a little thicker, strangers continued to perceive me as white until I went to college in New York City. If you're multi-racial, New York is easier to live in than Los Angeles because there's more diversity and less segregation. There, for the first time, I interacted with the Caribbean-American community and, noticing the cultural differences between blacks from the Caribbean and African Americans, I thought I began to understand why my mom insisted she was West Indian. More importantly, I shared subway cars and sidewalks with Puerto Ricans, Dominicans, Trinidadians, Mexicans—all of whom have a tradition of racial mixing.

New York Accepted Differences

I was no longer perceived as white. I'd become racially ambiguous. In airports I was, unfortunately, Middle Eastern. In the Italian section of Williamsburg, Brooklyn, I was Italian. In job interviews, after potential employers saw my last name, I was Jewish. In Spanish-owned delis, Puerto Rican. "Tres dólares," the woman at the register would say to me. Of course, this change came with its own burden. No longer racially fixed, people based assumptions about me on the clothes I wore, the people I walked with, the neighborhood I walked in. Still, because few people were sure what I was, I was rarely faced with overtly racist comments.

In October, when I moved back to Los Angeles, I finally learned why my mom had never let herself be labeled black. She, too, was multiracial. East Indian, French Creole, Scottish and, yes, African—all these bloods run in her veins. If she had told me before, I'd been too young to listen.

Gradually, between October and February, I realized that in all my attempts to wrestle down a racial identity, I'd learned that to be racially mixed is to be made up of a contradiction: your mom's race, your dad's race and, therefore, neither his nor hers. This is different than to repeat that line about race labels being false, to say that the labels "white" and "black" are theoretical. What feels real is real. It is to say that I will never be completely black. I will never be completely white. I may be West Indian, I may be Jewish, but, racially, I am forever an outsider. It is my place.

Being of Mixed Race in America

Eduardo Porter

Removed from American culture, mixed-race families lead a life in the shadows, according to the author. Comparing U.S. culture with that of his childhood in Mexico, he finds that being of mixed race in America is a stigma unknown in Mexico City, and he is hopeful that mixed-heritage families will be more visible in the United States in the future.

As a multiracial and somewhat foreign person I have on occasion found myself on the receiving end of the same kind of unease that many Americans seem to have about Barack Obama's ambiguous identity. He is either not black enough or too black. His name sounds odd. He had a weird childhood with kids who didn't speak English.

Mr. Obama is not just politically atypical. He is unusual demographically. A recent paper by economists from Harvard, Yale and the University of Chicago said that in 2000 only one in 70 births in the United States came from mixed, black-white parents. In the 1980s it was one in 200. In the 1960s, when Mr. Obama was born, there were virtually none.

Black-white teens are so rare today, the researchers argued, that they feel they have to engage in more risky behavior to be accepted by others: drink more, fight more, steal more, do illegal drugs more than either blacks or whites—a pattern of behavior known to social scientists as the "marginal man."

Racial Slotting

Perhaps this is true. Yet I would suggest that these outcomes say more about the context in which American multiracial

Eduardo Porter, "Contemplations on Being of Mixed Race in America," *The New York Times*, August 10, 2008. Reproduced by permission. http://www.nytimes.com/2008/08/11/opinion/11 mon4.html.

kids grow up than about the kids themselves. The United States practices cleanly defined racial slotting.

I'm not an avid TV watcher, but when I watch, the black man gets the black woman and whites date whites. I have yet to see an ad with a mixed-race family. Whites marry blacks, but rarely. Over all, 5.7 percent of married couples in 2000 crossed racial boundaries.

The American approach to race is unique, in a way. In Brazil, with a history of slavery and racism as brutal as America's, some 39 percent of the people define themselves as mixed race, or "pardos." By contrast, when the United States census in 2000 first allowed respondents to tick as many racial boxes as they wanted, only 2.4 percent ticked more than one. Never mind that genetic testing suggests a great deal of intermixing between Americans of African and European decent.

The son of a tallish, white father from Chicago and a short, brown Mexican mother of European and Indian blood, I'm not the same mix as Obama. As a colleague recently told me, I "read white." Growing up in Mexico City, where power and skin color correlate at least as well as in the United States, I led a privileged existence. Still, being a mix was never an issue; most of my peers were too.

Racial Politics

This is not to suggest Mexico has dealt with race any better. Racism just took different forms. European colonizers of modern-day Latin America encouraged the whitening of Indians and blacks. In the century after independence, ethnic loyalties were subsumed under a mixed Mexican identity as a way to merge Europeans and pre-Columbian indigenous nations into a modern Mexican state.

Today the Mexican census doesn't even ask about race, and it only started asking about indigenous ethnicity in 2000. José Vasconcelos, a politician and philosopher, wrote in the 1920s that Mexicans were of the "cosmic race"—that which included all others. Yet Mexico's state-sanctioned mestizo identity allowed its rulers to ignore its beleaguered indigenous populations—virtually defining them out of existence.

Insisting on Racial Boundaries

In the United States by contrast, racially inspired policies, whether they resulted in Jim Crow laws or affirmative action, fueled an urge to define and redefine hard racial boundaries. Close attention to race has forced uncomfortable issues of racial inequity into public debate, but has also gotten in the way of embracing a blended racial identity.

Fortunately, Americans seem to be slowly becoming more comfortable with racial intermingling. Newer immigrant groups with different experiences of race are already chipping away at the racial divide. About 10 percent of Asian Americans ticked two or more race boxes in the 2000 census. More than 15 percent of Hispanics marry non-Hispanics. And Hispanics are so confused about American racial categories that half of them can't find an appropriate race box on the census form and tick "other race" instead.

For all the mistrust of Mr. Obama's ancestry and ethnicity, he might even help this trend along, allowing blacks and whites to take a fresh look at each other. Then maybe people like me won't need to engage in extreme behaviors to fit in.

SOCIAL ISSUES
FIRSTHAND

CHAPTER 2

Parenting in Mixed-Heritage Families

Religion and Culture in a Mixed-Heritage Family

Dawn Friedman

Every religion and culture has its own set of values, its traditions and rituals. In the following essay, Dawn Friedman remarks on the challenge of bringing Judaism and Christianity together in her family, giving both religions their due without producing a meaningless blend. She also talks about the added demand of letting her adopted African American daughter experience traditions that are foreign to other members of the family. Dawn Friedman is a writer for Salon *and other publications.*

We are a transracial family. My husband, my son and myself are white. Our daughter is African-American and joined our family through an open, domestic adoption three years ago [in 2004]. Both my kids are being raised in my Jewish faith in that their formal religious education is happening at our synagogue. They are also being raised less formally with some understanding of Christianity because their father is a Christian. Because it's easier for me to talk about my beliefs than it is for their dad to talk about his, when my 10-year-old son asks big questions I answer from a Jewish perspective, as I understand it.

We're not so great at the trappings of either of our religions. Judaism—even Reform—has a lot of trappings and this is one of several reasons that our kids are at temple instead of at church. It's pretty easy to embrace Christianity—you just become Christian. But Judaism has a lot of formal rites that can be confusing and off-putting and to learn them now will make it easier for them to live Jewish later, if they choose to.

Dawn Friedman, "Religion and Culture in an Interfaith Transracial Family," AntiRacistParent.com, December 17, 2007. Reproduced by permission. http://www.antiracistparent.com/2007/12/17/religion-and-culture-in-an-interfaith-transracial-family/.

Learning Different Faiths

That's our immediate family: non-denominational, liberal Christian and very Reform Jew. Our extended families are everything from Christian Scientist to Atheist to Catholic to Pagan. My kids have some exposure to all of that, but their faith teachings spring from my Judaism and [my husband] Brett's Christianity.

Now to explain why I feel that it's more important that our daughter Madison have exposure to Christianity than it is for our son:

1. Her birth family is French-Catholic. Her grandparents met in Catholic high school (Her birth mom, Jessica, has a French last name that's very common in New Orleans). Madison's history on both her maternal and her paternal grandparents' side is Creole way, way back. She should have a cultural understanding of that because it's a rich part of her birth heritage.

2. Also her birth family, even when they don't practice Catholicism, does practice Christianity. It's a huge part of their lives and the emails and things we get from them reflect this. She needs to understand this so she has a shared language or at the very least understands their point of view. (Also as an aside, her adoption into a Jewish-identifying family was a concern for some of her first family, and we've made a point of letting them know that they don't need to censor their faith with us.)

3. Likewise, Christianity is a very important part of the African American community at large. "Church clothes," gospel music, biblical teachings—they are important cultural touchstones. Madison is going to miss out on a lot of cultural touchstones by virtue of growing up in our white family and I can't try to replicate them for her. What I can do is offer her an understanding of them by actively seeking out members of the community who are willing to educate her about them.

I don't think that Madison has a "true" religion that I can ferret out by looking at the color of her skin or her family tree. I certainly don't have the hubris to enter into the debate happening in the black community about the relevance of Christianity—what do I know? I'm a white Jew! I'm not talking about faith; I'm talking about the cultural experience of religion.

Making Sense of Cultures

We're all for formal and informal multicultural religious education and the informal part is, to me, about addressing the immediacy of a shared cultural experience. This is also why I haven't gone out of my way to expose my children to Buddhists—we don't know any. (We know some people who are casually interested in Buddhism but no one who is a practicing Buddhist.) Likewise, in my need-to-happen-more forays into the local African American community, I'm seeing a default to Christianity. Several black people have also explicitly told me that I need to expose Madison to Christianity.

A woman wrote me awhile back about being a Jewish woman with a child from Guatemala and she said that her son's birth religion is Catholic but she can't teach him Catholicism because she's Jewish. I understand the dilemma—but I'm NOT talking about raising our children in their birth faith. I'm talking about giving our children an understanding of their birth culture.

Keeping Culture and Faith Apart

Here's something of an example—one reason I think people assume I'm Christian is that I understand some Christian language. I understand what "the word" means. I understand what it means when someone says, "I was convicted on that." Recently a guy I met at a networking event assumed I was Christian after he used some of that language and I didn't ask him what he meant. I realize that by knowing his language, he was able to more comfortably (and surely unconsciously) make an assumption about me. I was welcome in a discussion we went on to have that I might not have been otherwise. I want Madison to *grok* [understand intuitively] the language.

It goes back to an old post I wrote about American-Family and math camp. To be Chinese, her Chinese husband quite clearly says, means to go to math camp. So should all white parents of adopted Chinese children sign up for math camp? Well, maybe. If math camp has the opportunity to be a shared touchstone that will make it easier for said child to enter into his/her birth community, then math camp has way more importance than just, you know, math camp. It's a cultural experience that can give a child options.

There are black kids at our synagogue (not many but they're there). The difference between them and Madison is that they all have at least one black parent. Those children may have to struggle to define what their blackness means to them (or what other people's assumptions about their blackness means to them) but it will be a different struggle than Madison's, and I think I need to be more proactive than those other parents need to be.

Growing Up Outside One's Birth Culture

I don't want to dictate Madison's experience by telling her that there is one more legitimate way to be black than another (that it is more legitimate to be Christian or Muslim or to embrace the example of Ethiopian Jews). Her experience as a child of African American heritage is legitimate because she is legitimate. *BUT* I do want her to know what the world at large is talking about. Even if she never has a chummy time in someone's kitchen getting her hair done, she needs to know that lots of other black women do and that sometimes people will look at her skin and think she shares an experience that she doesn't. I don't want her to be broadsided by this—I want her to be prepared, at the very least to be prepared to know that she doesn't know things but also where to find out. I want her to feel comfortable finding out. Having some shared language will, I know, make her search easier.

The reason I know how painful it is to be ignorant of things that feel like they should have been a birth right is that I'm a second generation interfaith Jew who converted at 30-something. It's hard sometimes to participate in temple activities and I can't help but wish my parents had given me an idea of what was going on even if they didn't want to teach me the faith of Judaism. (It's a relief to be able to talk about grandmother's hamantaschen even though I didn't even know that's what they were until I went to my first Purim celebration as an adult.) Sometimes I don't mind being ignorant but lots of times I want to (irony alert) pass as a regular old Jew. Sometimes Madison will want to be able to blend in, too, and I will do my best to open doors so she can craft her own identity instead of being stuck with the one we're foisting on her.

What Madison's faith will be is entirely up to her—she may end up feeling strong ties to her French-Catholic ancestry, or her adoptive dad's mom's Christian Science history, or she may say to heck with all that and become a Scientologist. Being a second-generation interfaith family, I feel that religion has way more to do with following your heart than with following familial dictates. But I also know that sometimes we look for—and find—truth by following our roots. Madison has a lot of roots. She has those that came to her by adoption, she has those that come from her first family and she has those that are part of the shared history of African Americans.

It's easy for me to share my faith and to share my family's faith (including her dad's family) but it will take special effort on my part to share the religious culture that she lost by being adopted. I want her to have access, should she choose to exercise it.

A Family Navigates Religious Obligations

Laura Lipman

To her dismay, the writer finds that the impending circumcision of her newborn son poses a problem for her family. Her husband, who doesn't share her Jewish faith, regards the ritual as brutal and questions its validity. In this selection, she addresses the struggles of keeping faith in a mixed-heritage family, but also speaks to the importance of making difficult decisions.

I hoped that I wouldn't have a boy. A girl would be so much easier—no *brit* [*milah*] [the covenant of circumcision].

"But why circumcision?" asked my quiet, red-headed, polite, of-Scottish-descent—in other words, not-Jewish—husband. As well he should, since we hadn't circumcised our first son when he was born.

Me: "But I wasn't involved in the Jewish community then. I'm in it now, we're raising our kids to be Jewish, they attend Jewish schools, we celebrate the Jewish holidays."

Him: "It's unnecessary, cruel and barbaric. Judaism's supposed to be so ethical, moral and civilized. Who's going to check, anyway?"

Me: "It's a way of welcoming a new male person into the tribe. It's a communal thing. Jews have done it for thousands of years. They're not any more violent or traumatized than anybody else."

Him: "This tribal stuff, that's the whole problem. It's the cause of so much violence, religious persecution, war, torture, suffering, inquisitions. My tribe's better than your tribe, so I'm going to kill you."

Laura Lipman, "Our Jewish Family: Two Sons, One Circumcized and One Not, A Scottish, Presbyterian Husband (Who Is Circumcized), and Me, the Jewish Mother," InterfaithFamily.com, June 29, 2005. Reproduced by permission. http://www.interfaithfamily.com/life_cycle/birth_ceremonies/Two_Sons_One_Circumcised_and_One_Not_A_Scottish_Presbyterian_Husband_(Who_is_Circumcised)_and_Me_the_Jewish_Mother.shtml?rd=1.

Between Emotion and Tradition

I remember this conversation and many more in the months of my pregnancy. Sometimes, in a haze of hormones and mother love, I could barely consider circumcision either. Other times, I felt that elemental pull of tradition impelling me to adopt more Jewish rituals in my life. The tug on the soul that led me down this path was leading me into the primeval heart of my people. I asked every Jewish mother I met about her experience with circumcision. Even the most unobservant circumcised their sons. It seemed unthinkable to them not to circumcise, even though they would never consider keeping *kosher* [adhering to Jewish dietary laws] or going to a *mukvah* (ritual bath) or observing any of the other 613 *mitzvot*, or commandments.

This is one *mitzvah* that most of us seem to have remembered with great clarity from that moment standing at Mt. Sinai.

"We wanted him to look like his dad, of course," one friend said.

"It has to do with cleanliness," said another.

"My parents insisted," another friend explained.

But our older son never once mentioned that he looked different from his dad. After all, the obvious difference was size, not foreskin. He never once had a urinary tract infection. And my parents would never insist; they were simply happy that I was returning to Judaism; after my years of New Age searching, they didn't really care what form my Judaism took. They, too, accepted circumcision unquestioningly, even though they were totally secular in every other way. What was it about circumcision that forced us beyond science, beyond reason, to embrace this elemental, blood ritual that seemed to define us as a people throughout our history? It became hard for me to defend this aspect of my religion to my husband; as a woman, how could I know what he would or wouldn't experience?

Circumcision Seemed Too Much

The complexities of Jewish law and communal practice were not what my husband bargained for sixteen years ago when we were first married. I became observant fairly suddenly about a year after our first son was born, and changed all the rules on him after the game had already started. Not easy, but he could see how wonderful Judaism was for our older son; the holidays, the *shul* [synagogue] we belong to, the schools. But circumcision just seemed to be too much, too final, too Jewish.

Would I still be a good Jew if I didn't circumcise my son? The circumcision of the infant is the father's obligation. If there is no father or the father is unwilling, it is the obligation of the *beit din*, or rabbinical court. And what if there is no *beit din*, but only a very tense, hysterical mother? I comforted myself with the idea that if I can't do this one mitzvah, there are 612 others.

My internal dialogue became saturated with thinking about *brit milah* circumcision. Do we observe without questioning? Can we pick and choose which commandments we want to observe, take the easy ones and toss out the politically incorrect or difficult ones? What about *kavannah* (intention)? Some people choose to observe the ritual of circumcision without the actual cutting. But to me that felt like cheating.

There was something about Jewish ritual that commanded that you actually do it, not sanitize it or spiritualize it. Certainly one can think about commandments and study and pray and question, but the thing itself has to be done, whether it's *tzedakah*, (giving charity), lighting *Shabbat*, or Sabbath, candles or *brit milah*, circumcision. In fact, *brit milah* really symbolized a quality that I craved in my spiritual searches—the bridging of the bitter and the sweet, heaven and earth, being and doing. It's the *charoset* (Passover dish of apples and honey) and the horseradish, the sweetness of birth and the pain of the milah.

What I began to realize was how Jewish my life had become. Even married to a non-Jew, I felt I was living as rich and full a Jewish life as I could. I was managing this incredible balancing act. Part of what helped was belonging to a wonderful, Modern Orthodox shul, or *synagogue*. What also helped was that we did not live near my husband's family (they were involved only peripherally in our lives), and they knew nothing of our dilemma.

"Everyone's circumcised now, it's not a symbol of being Jewish anymore," my husband added in amazement and perplexity as it seemed that I would not compromise on this one.

"We're living Jewish lives, this will make it easier for him as he grows up. I want this for him," I answered.

As it turned out, the decision seemed to be made, somewhat mysteriously, through God's grace, or our love for one another, or through sheer exhaustion. My husband acquiesced, not totally understanding, not knowing why, but I would have to attribute his decision to the strength of his love for me and our children and this sometimes strange entity that is our family.

So we have two sons, one circumcised, one not, a father who is not Jewish but is circumcised, and we are a Jewish family. Sometimes I relish this experiment that is our Jewish family, sometimes I wish it could be easier.

Religious Acceptance Makes the December Holidays Fun

David Pedrick

Sometimes, the reason for holiday celebrations can get lost in the December shopping whirlwind, but the author, whose family shares two faiths, insists that the festivities can be shared among those of differing religions. Writing about his own background and about the challenge to stay true to both Judaism and Christianity, he embraces differences and commonalities alike.

As a Unitarian Universalist congregation, we tend to be more open than many people about religious pluralism. Nevertheless, with the coincidence of Christmas and Chanukah in [December], religious differences come into unavoidable focus. Several of our families are interfaith, each of which will have its own ways of incorporating these differences. As a Unitarian Universalist with a Jewish family through marriage, I'd like to share a few experiences and perspectives that Laura and our children, Ben and Geoff, have incorporated into our interfaith family life.

When Laura and I were preparing for marriage more than 20 years ago, we asked some interfaith couple friends about what concerns to anticipate. One light-hearted reply was that it is easy to sort out which in-laws to be with for the holidays. On a more serious note, the genuine acceptance of practices other than one's own is fundamental in interfaith life.

Acceptance vs. Tolerance

I emphasize the word "acceptance." It has quite a different characteristic than tolerance, which George Washington recognized during his visit to Newport in 1790. He came to assure

David Pedrick, "Celebrating Traditions in Untraditional Ways—Some Interfaith Family Views in the Holiday Season," ChanningChurch.org, December 4, 2005. Reproduced by permission. http://www.channingchurch.org/Archives/Talks/2005/12-4_Pedrick.html.

the people of Rhode Island, which had only just signed on guardedly as the 13th state, that their well-established practice of freedom of religion would be upheld in the new nation. Moses Seixas, the congregation leader of Touro Synagogue, welcomed Washington with a letter that referred to "a Government, which to bigotry gives no sanction, to persecution no assistance—but generously affording ... Liberty of conscience [to] everyone, of whatever Nation, tongue or language." Washington drew from Seixas's letter in his reply a few days later "To the Hebrew Congregation in Newport," going further to say that "It is no more that toleration is spoken of, as if it was by the indulgence of one class of people, that another enjoyed the exercise of their inherent natural rights."

These elegant and historic words were penned within footsteps of where we sit today, but sadly, in the course of more than two centuries, their broadly spoken message still doesn't ring easily among many people. It has been difficult enough to reach a level of toleration among different peoples and religions. It's another significant step to achieve mutual acceptance.

Laura and I had a very special surprise in our wedding ceremony that was known only to the officiating rabbi and us. It had been made clear to me that the service could not be modified to integrate my Episcopalian tradition, other than as a written insert in the program. Each of the Jewish wedding prayer endings, where the Christian words familiar to me would have been, ". . . in the name of the Father, Son and Holy Spirit," ended as, ". . . in the name of the people of Israel." In our conversations with the rabbi leading up to the wedding, I commented that those words struck me as very Jewish until I reconciled my comfort level through realizing that Christianity and Christian followers reach back to their roots in Israel through Jewish heritage. The rabbi absorbed Laura's and my interfaith comfort, and, without saying anything beforehand, changed the prayer endings at our wedding to, ". . . in mutual religious respect."

Living Mutual Respect

The principle of mutual religious respect underscores the way that Laura and I have enjoyed our lives together. There has been no expectation that one would change who we are, just to be more like the other. Instead, we have incorporated each other's traditions into our family life. In our respective practices, Laura found a fulfilling religious home at Touro Synagogue, where our two sons have received their Jewish education and been stellar Bar Mitzvahs, and Laura has been serving as the congregation president. I continued originally as an Episcopalian, but found that the values and practices of Unitarian Universalism at Channing were really more consistent with my personal beliefs. Through our respective paths, my family has enjoyed the richness of our differing traditions and beliefs, while maintaining our core, shared values.

The introductory years to each other's holidays did take some getting used to. At my first Passover Seder at Laura's parents' home—with about thirty family and close friends, many of whom I was meeting for the first time—of course I got the two longest readings of the Haggadah [seder meal readings]. Christmas in Vermont with my brother's and sister's families, who go over the top on presents and decorations, has been a lot for Laura to get used to. But both of these holidays, which each celebrate a historical episode in their respective religions, are wonderful, joyous family highlights of the year.

Chanukah is actually a minor Jewish holiday. It's become more conspicuous because of its timing near Christmas. Also called the Festival of Lights, Chanukah is based on the miracle story of a lamp that burned for eight days on limited oil. Holiday foods cooked in oil—especially potato latkes—are a symbol of that. Gifts had nothing to do with Chanukah until the Christmas holiday spilled over into it. In our house, we do exchange some Chanukah presents, but the focus is on the lighting of the candles in our three Menorahs—one each for Laura, Ben and Geoff—saying the prayers in Hebrew and singing Chanukah songs. On one of the nights we have a small Chanukah party at our house with latkes and other foods. One of our well-established traditions is Geoff's good friend Ben Fernandez, who has been part of our Chanukah celebration for longer than I can remember.

Sharing Different Joy

As hard as it may be to get past the in-your-face commercialism of Christmas advertising, music and store displays for six weeks or so, there are some familiar pleasures that Christmas and Chanukah both bring. Lights are a beautiful sight, whether they be the glow of candles in a Menorah, lights in windows and outdoors on trees and houses, or on a Christmas tree. Both holidays commemorate their respective miracles, and have legends and observances that have grown from those miracles. Both holidays ring with music and bring family and friends together with great joy in people's hearts. And, yes, there is the excitement of presents given and received.

The many pleasures of the holidays are there to be shared and enjoyed. At the same time, their religious basis shouldn't be lost in the celebratory excitement, although everyone can choose how much to read into the specific religious aspects of a given holiday. As we read together [at a religious service], ". . . And the people of the earth will be glad, and celebrate each in their own ways."

My Kids Are Biracial

Debra J. Dickerson

In this selection, a black mother has to answer her small children's first questions about the difference between their skin color and hers. She acknowledges that her biracial children cannot be exclusively claimed by either white or black communities, but she asserts that they are part of both. Debra J. Dickerson is the author of The End of Blackness *and* An American Story.

Out of the blue last week my son, who is 5, asked me if I'd ever been "burned." I thought he was referring to the tattoos that I always tell him and his sister are boo-boos (how else to justify voluntary scarring when I won't even let them use a butter knife?), so I repeated my usual lie and added that "Mommy would *never* play with fire." I thought this was a safety discussion. He looked confused.

"Oh. I thought that was why you were brown."

My biracial, white-looking baby is discovering race. Granted, both of my children think my nappy, unprocessed, Sideshow Bob hair looks that way simply to entertain them, and never understand why everyone asks if I'm their nanny. I can't say I wasn't on notice. But I'd envied them their racial innocence. Too bad them days are over.

My son first brought up the subject of race two months ago. I took him and his 3-year-old sister to a concert at an inner-city elementary school right before Christmas. There were lots of cornrowed kids singing "Jingle Bells." My own child, as he sat fidgeting in my lap, stared at the crowd around him goggle-eyed and perplexed.

"Mommy," he said, craning his neck to scan the room, just so he could be certain, "everybody's brown. Really, look! They're all brown."

Debra J. Dickerson, "Don't Be Black on My Account," Salon.com, March 5, 2007. This article first appeared in Salon.com, at http://www.salon.com. An online version remains in the Salon archives. Reprinted with permission.

We live in snow-white upstate New York, but was he really so clueless?

"Why is everybody brown, Mommy?"

Yup. He was. Caught unawares, I just gulped for air. But he was waiting for an answer.

"Really, Mom. *Everyone's* brown. Everyone. Why?"

Finally, I responded. "Mommy's brown, honey," I said, and I covered his hand with my own. "See?"

Discovering Race

This did not compute. He blinked at me a few times and went back to squirming around and checking out all the brown people in the room.

The music was playing but his questions continued. I talked about how, like Mommy, these people had two brown parents while he and his sister had a brown mom and a . . . "not brown" dad. (My kids are not brown at all; homie's blond and his sister has waist-length ringlets with natural blond highlights.) I told him that he and his sister would likely get "browner" as they got older and talked about variety being the spice of life. I analogized from the many colors in his paint box and reminded him that his Grandma Johnnie was brown but that his Grandma Ruth was . . . not brown. Then, I took a deep breath and laid it on him.

"Honey. You're black. Did you know that?"

And even as the words left my mouth, I knew they made no sense. He was talking skin color, I was talking politics.

Hopelessly lost now, he just gaped up at me. Then he pulled his black clip-on tie from his sweater and said, helpfully, "My tie is black." Still wriggling on his brown mommy's lap, he went back to staring in confused wonderment at all the Negroes.

Color and Politics

Now, two months later, he has come up with an explanation. "They" are all brown because "they" are irresponsible with flammables. I know I need to nip this in the bud. But how on earth do you explain things as complicated as race and blackness to creatures who believe that the police will know when we need help because they all have baby monitors in their cars? They're so young; I'm still in the gooey, overprotective stage of motherhood wherein I shield them from knowing about crime, homelessness, war, rape, pedophilia and the horrors of capitalism. But I'm supposed to tell them that white people, their father's people, enslaved, raped, sold and Jim Crow'd us simply because we look burned all over? And I'm supposed to tell them now, when my 3-year-old daughter is still oblivious to the whole subject of race, that racism is far, far from over? Even if I wanted to tell them all this, I'm not sure where I'd start.

And then, last night, while still meditating on my son's burn theory, I located the true source of my ambivalence about helping my children discover their blackness.

Like most kids, mine love to "give me five" to signal any sort of triumph. Last night, I realized that I'd stifled a reflexive impulse to teach them part of the high-five—"on the black hand side." Back in the militant '60s and early '70s when I was a kid, black men would often slap each other five, then flip their hands over and do it again on "the black hand side" or "the black man's side." Now it's rarely done and only then as kitsch, but what explains my hesitance, my refusal, to initiate my children into the club when this relic of my identity formation naturally surfaced? As I thought about that, all at once it hit me that I never "talk black" with my kids either. None of the "used ta coulds" and "mighta woulds" and "he be's" that I slip into so comfortably with my Miss'ippi mama and relatives back home. Without realizing it, I had made Chez Debra Ebonics-free [Ebonics is African American vernacular English] when the kids were in earshot, even though my bilingualism has been the key to my mainstream success. So why wasn't I teaching *them* to be bilingual? Why was I refusing them their ghetto pass?

Being Black vs. Acting Black

If I'm honest, I know why. It's because I know they're not black. I am but they're not. They're biracial.

I *lived* blackness. All they can do is *study* and *perform* blackness. My parents were Mississippi sharecroppers who became part of the Great Migration north. My great-grandfather, who lived well past 100 and was still kicking when I was a child, had been born a slave. *His* son, my grandfather, got a "Klan escort" out of Mississippi. I saw "Whites only" signs when we went visiting down south and remembered white cops coming to my A'int Mazelle's to "urge" her to teach her kin from up north in St. Louis "how to behave." Clueless, I hadn't yielded my place in line to whites at the country store. At my own home in Missouri I knew not to enter South St. Louis after dark, and I grew up sharing my World War II combat veteran father's bitterness at the racism of the Marine Corps. Segregation made black culture pervasive in our lives; the same oppression that so limited our options gave us all a common frame of reference. My kids can only study that in books.

I never make them the soul food I grew up eating—it's so unhealthy, however heavenly. Besides, I only know how to make cornbread and cabbage for eight. I live far, far from my relatives; my kids have spent far more time with their relatives on their father's side because travel is foreign, and too expensive, for my working-class family. I lasted only a few Sundays taking my kids to a black Southern Baptist church like the one I attended growing up because I couldn't, in good conscience, give my implicit stamp of approval to all that drove me away in the first place. We belong to a Unitarian church now, though I deeply miss gospel music. Had the kids and I stayed in D.C. things might be different, but now that we live in upstate New York, we encounter very few black people and even fewer who are not mainstream professionals, with all the requisite class implications that follow (affluent, private-school educated, i.e., not very culturally black).

Cultural Tourists

I can't bring myself to turn my kids into cultural tourists of their mother's people by, for example, sending them to black church camps during the summer, like some of my bougie [bourgeois] black friends have done. Blacks are not exotic creatures to be visited on brief safaris. How could I ever make my daughter understand why I wept through "The Color Purple" on Broadway a few weeks ago? Truth be told, I don't even *want* her to understand how cathartic that was for someone born a poor and very black woman. I don't want to force experiences on my son and daughter just to make them feel black. And that's not because they look white. It's because they're half-white, features be damned.

As much as blacks bemoan the "one drop rule," no one works harder to enforce it and keep it alive. See: blacks' attitude toward Tiger Woods. I thought he was as much a self-hating sellout as most blacks did with his "Cablinasian" routine. Then, I heard him say that he didn't consider himself solely black because it was an insult to his mother. That nearly blew a hole in my brain. He's absolutely right—it *is* an insult to the mother who carried him, birthed him in agony and raised him. Why on earth should her Thai heritage count for nothing and his dad's black heritage count for everything? If my children ever self-identify as "white" I'll be crushed. That would be tantamount to saying all my love and sacrifice and devotion meant nothing. Mrs. Woods is not a brood mare and neither am I. If my kids end up identifying as "black" rather than white or biracial, I'll be secretly pleased. But in the end, if they can go toe to toe with me, they can consider themselves whatever they like.

Giving Kids a Choice

Given the level of intellectual and moral rigor to which I plan to hold my children, I can't in good conscience as a human being tell them which category to pick, if any. If that means they prefer sushi to fried catfish, so be it. If they prefer Europe to Africa, if they're consumed by environmentalism but not civil rights, fine. Since my son recently whined about wanting a bigger house and blithely opined that "everyone has a car," I'm more focused on teaching them about class and injustice than race right now. Still, I dug out all the old family photos of my Jim Crow ancestors to teach them about their forebears as individuals, not via their relationship to whites (that will come later). I've also invested in books like "I Like Myself," "The Skin I'm In" and "The Colors of Us" to teach them about all the variations in the human race and among people of color. I want them to understand that their lives will be enriched by diversity, not by forced field trips to where the Negroes live. We break out the globe frequently and I teach them about Africa and England, the two places I know figure in my bloodline. I ask them to get Daddy to tell them about their Scottish and Norwegian heritage, but I doubt he does. No matter, the world will teach them about their whiteness.

My attitude on all this will undoubtedly evolve with time and my kids will come home with more and more questions about being black. I still don't know what to do with the more exclusionary facets of our culture, like Ebonics or "on the black man's side." I don't know whether I'm begrudging them their blackness or sparing them baggage that might hold them back, but we've got time. I look forward to it, because, like the T shirt says, if you love something, set it free. I grew up black. They're growing up multiracial citizens of the world, born to two cultures, neither more worthy or intrinsically interesting than the other. Because passing for black is no better than passing for white.

My Mixed-Race Family Is a Testament to Change

Diane Bartz

Mixed marriages were a social taboo when her grandparents were growing up, but Diane Bartz sees a change in America's attitude toward race. She describes how her own father underwent a transformation once he was confronted with biracial grandchildren. Diane Bartz writes for Reuters news service, covering antitrust and patent litigation.

When my father was growing up in a Minnesota farm town during the Depression, his German Lutheran mother vehemently opposed mixed marriages. For her, that included her son marrying someone of Norwegian descent. Or a Catholic.

Now, my father, who is white, has two white grandchildren, two who have a black father and two adopted from Asia.

To me, the fact that Armin Bartz adores his white, light brown and dark brown grandchildren is testament to how much America has changed in the past 70 years.

His youth—like that of many older Americans—was in a rural, agricultural America where a 20-mile trip was difficult and unusual. Contact with different ethnic groups was sporadic at best.

He tells of a tense Thanksgiving Day dinner at the home of some cousins, a farmer named Wilmer Radel and his red-headed Catholic wife Katherine Ryan—especially when Katherine mentioned the Virgin Mary in a prayer.

"My parents before going out there talked about it, wondering how Wilmer and Katherine were going to handle the prayer. So that increased my interest and ramped up the tension," my father, who is 77, told me.

This was not an America where someone like Barack Obama, son of a white Kansas woman and a black man from Kenya, could be a serious presidential candidate.

My sister Pam was the first to have children, giving birth to two girls. But then my father learned that his daughter Lisa, whose partner is black, was pregnant. And he feared that he would not adore the baby as he did the older two grandchildren.

Getting over Prejudice

He admitted he was afraid of what people would think, and that he was a little embarrassed.

But everything changed when the baby was born. "I think Jordan's a handsome little boy. Once I start to interact with him, it all goes away," he said of Lisa's oldest, now 12.

It was only in 1967 that the Supreme Court, in its ruling *Loving v. Virginia*, struck down the last of the U.S. laws designed to prevent black and white Americans from marrying [each other].

Lisa, who lives in Minnesota, said that she never worried about our father's reaction, but she would have feared what her grandparents might have said.

"The immediate family I didn't worry about," she told me, adding that she remembered my dad chastising one of her friends for using a racial slur.

Just a "Boring" Family

Interestingly, Jordan identifies himself as black while his sister Eva, 7, sees herself as more biracial.

My sister says her family is "boring"—except for the fact that her partner cooks while she does most of the yard work.

"We do all the normal stuff that everyone else in the neighborhood does. We go to work, come home and take the kids to sports," she said.

The family got even more complicated when I, then single, went to China in 2001 to adopt a child and to India three years later to adopt a toddler who is darker than most African-Americans.

I soon found out that multiracial families have tensions I never expected.

One is that of the kids themselves, who want to be just like parents whom they don't resemble a whit. My younger daughter once tried to scratch off her brown skin with her fingernail so that she could be white like me. She didn't stop until she bled.

But my parents have been everything I'd hoped for as grandparents to my kids.

On a last visit to Minnesota, my children were fed their favorite foods, introduced to polka music and told fanciful stories of leprechauns who drop quarters from the ceiling.

But that doesn't mean my dad is completely at home in a multiracial America.

When he goes to Jordan's American football and basketball games, he feels uncomfortable—not because he thinks poorly of anyone else but because he fears they will assume—because of his age—that he is a racist. And perhaps they fear that he is making negative assumptions about them.

"When I see my (white) neighbor working on his car, I go up to him and say, 'Do you know what you're doing?'" said my dad, who has a dry sense of humor. "I wouldn't dare do that . . . with black people."

CHAPTER 3

Mixed Heritage in a
Multicultural Society

Everyone Asks About My Racial Background

Elliott Lewis

While on assignment in a homeless shelter, television journalist Elliott Lewis is asked about his racial background and has to confront the lingering suspicions people have when he says that he is biracial. No community will fully claim him as one of their own, but Lewis realizes that definitions of race and skin color and people's attitudes toward them have always been in flux. He realizes that he may yet find his own place in American society. Lewis is a broadcast journalist.

"Can I ask you something?" the man said.

"Sure," I said.

"What is your racial background?"

Here we go again, I thought.

It was Thanksgiving Day, 1996. I was working as a reporter at WKMG-TV, the CBS affiliate in Orlando, Florida. I had just arrived at the local homeless shelter to prepare a report on a holiday tradition. Volunteers from throughout the community had gathered to serve up hundreds of free turkey dinners to those in need.

That's the story I was covering. But at that moment, a black man at the homeless shelter was the one asking the questions.

"What is your racial background?" he wanted to know.

That question has dogged me for as long as I can remember. As a child, I wasn't quite sure what to say. Now, after years of practice, I've developed a standard answer.

Elliott Lewis, *Fade: My Journeys in Multiracial America*, New York: Carroll and Graf, 2006. Copyright © 2006 by Elliott Lewis. Reprinted by permission of Avalon Publishing a member of Perseus Books, L.L.C.

"I'm biracial," I told him.

"So that means what?" he asked, his face contorting as if he'd never heard the term before.

"I'm a mixture of black and white," I continued.

"Oh . . . just curious," he said. Then he changed the subject.

Living Biracial

No more than five minutes later, another black man at the shelter called me over to his table. I thought he was going to ask not to have his picture taken, or ask me what time he might be on the news, or try to give me a tip on a possible story. That's usually what happened whenever I visited homeless shelters before. But he had something else on his mind.

"Hey, are you black?" he blurted out.

Before I could even answer, the man spoke up again.

"You're sort of black. Aren't you? Sort of?"

"I'm biracial," I said, trying to act casual. "I'm both black and white."

At this point, I was beginning to wonder how many times I would have to go through this little interrogation before the day was over. That's when the third black man approached me.

"I was just wondering," he began. "What race are you?"

Maybe I should just wear a sign around my neck. "I'm biracial. Get over it." Or, "Stop staring. I'm mixed race." Or, better yet, "It's a multiracial thing. You wouldn't understand."

Changing the U.S. Census

But that was before the U.S. Census Bureau took a significant step toward reshaping how many Americans think about race and racial labeling. The 2000 census marked the first time in U.S. history that Americans had the option to check more than one racial category in the official government head count. Whereas previous census forms had instructed respondents to "check only one" racial category, the directions on the form used in 2000 read, "Mark one or more races to indicate what this person considers himself/herself to be." Nearly seven million Americans checked more than one box on their questionnaire. News organizations around the country took notice, sparking numerous articles examining this "new" population and delving into why we chose to identify ourselves the way we did.

The media exposure has brought more attention to the existence of interracial families in the United States and created more awareness of the dynamics of multiracial identity issues. But even in a post–Census 2000 world, old attitudes, misunderstandings, and outdated models of thinking about our identity choices persist. We've also had our share of disagreements within Interracial Family Circles over many of these issues and the public policy implications of formally recognizing those who identify with more than one race.

Nevertheless, if there is one universal experience commonly cited among those who have embraced a multiracial identity, it is the frequency with which we are asked the "What are you?" question. We are constantly called upon to either explain what others perceive as our ambiguous racial appearance, or to choose sides and declare an allegiance to one ethnic group over another. Meanwhile, those biracial people whose looks are more easily aligned with traditional, single-race categories do not face such interrogation to nearly the same degree. "I can't racially classify you, and it's bothering me," the questioners seem to be saying, "so tell me what you are so I can figure out which box to put you in and determine how to relate to you."

Choosing a Box

The easy thing for me to do would be to say that I am black. Period. End of story. And leave it at that. That's what many people would still prefer that I do. Their argument goes something like this: even if you're only part-black, our race-conscious society will judge you to be all-black and treat you accordingly. So you might as well just say you're black, get used to it, and move on with your life.

I've been called the N-word enough times to know that argument has some validity. I also know that while being biracial doesn't grant anyone immunity from racial discrimination, it doesn't necessarily make someone "all-black, all the time" in society's eyes, either. If it did, then those black men at the homeless shelter wouldn't have spent so much time wondering out loud, "Hey, what are you?" The fact that the question even arises tells me there is a considerable degree of uncertainty over just how "black" I am.

Thanksgiving Day at the homeless shelter was certainly not the first time in my television career that I'd faced questions about my racial identity. It started years earlier in Reno, Nevada, the twenty-four-hour gambling town in the shadow of the Sierra Nevada that the local tourism industry has branded "The Biggest Little City in the World." I had worked at KTVN-TV, Reno's CBS affiliate, as an unpaid intern while in college. Six months later, in January 1988, I joined the staff as an on-air reporter. I worked the night shift, appearing on the station's 11 p.m. newscast, and covered everything from homicides to house fires, from sex scandals to school board meetings.

Adjusting the Color on the TV

The white news director who hired me (at a whopping salary of $14,000 a year) predicted that one day I might have a prosperous television career in a city such as New Orleans. With its large Creole population, he reasoned, a newscaster with my skin color would appeal to black viewers while being light enough to not drive away racist white viewers. So far, my television career has taken me to six different cities: Reno, San

Diego, Portland (Oregon), Cincinnati, Orlando, and Washington, D.C. I have never been offered a job in New Orleans.

I was still learning my way around northern Nevada when a news photographer I was working with brought up the race issue. We had just finished shooting our last story of the night and were on our way back to the station. Scotty, a nervous, blond-haired, middle-aged white guy who often paced the newsroom holding a portable police scanner up to his ear, mentioned that a friend of his had seen me on the air the night before.

"Funny thing," Scotty began. "This guy was telling me how he ended up adjusting the color on his television set while you were on, because he couldn't figure out what you were. . . . Didn't know whether you were white, black, Hispanic, or what!"

I rolled my eyes. "He doesn't need to adjust his TV," I said as our white Jeep Cherokee pulled up to the station. "Hasn't he ever seen a biracial person before?"

Multiracial people certainly aren't anything new. Miscegenation—a word once commonly used to refer to "race-mixing"—has been going on for some time. As University of California sociologist Reginald Daniel told *The New Yorker*, "In my family, like many families with African American ancestry, there is a history of multiracial offspring associated with rape and concubinage."

Family Trees Are Diverse

"The legacy of this intermingling," concluded the magazine, "is that Americans who are descendants of early settlers, of slaves, or of Indians often have ancestors of different races in their family tree."

That being the case, it would seem just about anyone nowadays could claim with some legitimacy to be multiracial or to come from an interracial family. But what I'm talking about here goes beyond having an intellectual understanding about being racially mixed. And it goes beyond the scientific arguments put forth recently that, biologically speaking, "race" does not exist.

This [viewpoint] is about those of us for whom being multiracial is part of our self-identity. We simply don't think of ourselves as belonging to only one "race," as contemporary American society—for better or worse—has come to use that term today. Our blended heritage is a part of our lives in a way that cannot be easily dismissed. The effect on our upbringing has been too profound for us to ignore. We come from families where the racial fault lines are exposed. Our ideas about who we are have been shaped by this peculiar racial dilemma and the various ways it plays itself out in our daily lives.

Racial blending has been going on in my family for generations. My mother, born Betty Jean Dent, is one of ten children, the products of a dark-skinned African-American father and a light-complexioned mother whom some neighbors mistook for Italian. In reality, my grandmother was a mix of black and white with perhaps some Native American thrown in. My mother's nine siblings—two brothers and seven sisters—display every shade of brown on the spectrum. My mom is one of the lightest in her family, and she married a light-skinned man.

My father, Coleman Alderson Lewis Jr., grew up as an only child, the son of a white woman and a self-identified black man. I say "self-identified" because in looking at old photos of my grandfather, I see a man with honey brown skin and straight black hair, which in my mind only raises more questions about when the racial lines in the family tree first got crossed.

Skin Color and Culture

In some respects, my parents are representative of the vast majority of African-Americans who are "multiracial by birth, but black through life experience." Their multiracial heritage is apparent. But their upbringing, social interactions, physical features, and other factors have led them to identify racially as "black." While estimates on the number of people who fall into that category vary, some researchers suggest up to 80 percent or more of America's "black" population have known white or Native American ancestry. But ancestry and identity are not necessarily the same thing.

"Under the law, we were black," my mother would say when describing the racial classification system she's known for most of her life. Having grown up at a time when public accommodations remained segregated and opportunities for people of color were severely limited, that "legal" identity was all that mattered. Although my mother attended a small, integrated high school in western Pennsylvania, what little integration there was in the late 1940s only went so far. When she tried out for the cheerleading squad, she didn't make the cut, "because black girls never got picked for cheerleader," she often told me. When my father decided to go to college in the 1930s, he enrolled in what is now Virginia State University. But his diploma from that institution bears its former name: Virginia State College for Negroes.

Color vs. Heritage

My parents' legal status as black people defined their lives in ways that are unimaginable to me. They identified as black in accordance with the rigid social customs in place in their communities and throughout the nation at the time. They would tell you there was no point in identifying otherwise, even if it had occurred to them—which I gather it never did. The idea that their racial identities might also serve as a personal statement expressing the fullness of their heritage was a foreign concept. The law was the law, and that was their reality.

For me, it has never been quite that simple. I am not only "multiracial by birth," but "multiracial through life experience," too. Taken together, the defining moments in my life have led me to think of myself as biracial. Born in 1966 and raised in a post–civil rights culture that championed integration, "color blindness," and later, "multiculturalism," any legal definition of blackness that may have existed carried less weight for me than for my parents. In my world, ideas about who is black and who isn't haven't been as clear-cut. Is pop singer Mariah Carey black? What about golfer Tiger Woods? Or actor Vin Diesel? What about me? The answers vary depending on whom you ask.

In the United States, we often think of race as something permanent, unbending, and indisputable. But the older I got, the more I traveled, and the more social encounters I had, the more I came to realize how societal views of race can fluctuate. Those views change across time, cultures, countries, geographic regions, generations, and even academic disciplines. Racial definitions—particularly for people with my shade of skin—are not set in stone; they're shifty, fluid, and evolving.

This fuzziness surrounding racial labels is a difficult thing for some people to grasp. But it's key to understanding the range of experiences multiracial people go through and the effect on our self-concept. To fully describe how I've come to terms with my racial identity and where I see myself in society today requires a longer, deeper, and more thoughtful discussion than most people have time for in everyday conversation. It's complex, and it took me more than twenty years to make sense of it all myself.

More than Skin Color

To understand that journey requires killing off some preconceived notions many people have about how identity is formed. First among these misconceptions is that my racial identity should be the same as that of my parents, since both of them also have interracial backgrounds. Well, it doesn't work that way. A mixed-race person born in the 1930s is bound to have different racial experiences than a biracial person born in the 1960s, who will in turn likely have different racial experiences than a biracial person growing up today. Those experiences are pivotal in shaping our racial identity choices—and the degree to which we feel we even have a choice in the first place.

Perhaps the most offensive misconception to me is that in saying "I'm biracial" I am in some way attempting to avoid being "stigmatized," that I somehow view being black as negative, bad, or distasteful, and that I'm trying to distance myself from a part of my heritage I don't like. I identify as biracial because, if I must choose a single racial label, then "biracial" is the one that fits me best given the totality of my life experience.

Flipping the Script

But no matter which racial label we select, trying to explain the dynamics of identity formation to someone unfamiliar with these issues can be a frustrating exercise—unless that person is willing to let go of their assumptions about multiracial people and approach the subject with an open mind. In the words of Roosevelt University sociologist Heather Dalmage, "We need to 'flip the script' and analyze why racial categories have been created in particular ways," and why certain people who identity themselves with only one race feel they have the right to pass judgment on multiracial people and their families. Friends, strangers, co-workers, even some of our own relatives claim they "can't figure us out," when in reality their own biases have clouded their interpretation of the defining moments in our lives and why we identify the way we do.

Understanding the multiracial experience requires a shift in perspective. It requires making an effort to walk in our shoes, to see the racial encounters in our lives as we have experienced them. Otherwise, biracial people will continue to be misunderstood.

Long before my professional life in front of a television camera began, I knew I was different. Certainly different from white folks, but also different from black folks. I learned this from various people I now refer to as "the Messengers of Miscegenation"—individuals who in one way or another served to remind me of my blended background and the resulting ambiguity of my racial appearance.

The messenger who had the most profound impact on me was my uncle Eugene. Of my mother's nine brothers and sisters, Eugene is one of the darker-skinned. One night at a family gathering, when I was somewhere between ten and twelve years old, my mother took me over to meet him. I was too young to remember the last time I'd seen Uncle Eugene, so when Mom introduced us, I expected him to say something like, "Man, how you've grown!" Or "Gosh, the last time I saw you, you were still sucking on a bottle"—one of those tired, cliché responses children typically hear from older relatives they haven't seen in a long time.

But when Uncle Eugene's eyes met mine, he didn't say a word to me. Instead, he turned to my mother and asked in a booming voice, "Betty, where did you get this white boy from?"

My Black Identity

Cord Jefferson

When the author hears the question, "Cord, are you black?" upon starting to work for a black blog, he first wants to answer that it is nobody's business. But he explains why his parents' heritage—he is white, black, and Native American—does not define him as much as people's reactions to his skin and hair. In a racially divided culture, he has come to embrace his "blackness."

On my first day at Stereohyped, I was asked by some readers what qualified me to work at the Web's most incisive black blog (ie "What's your race?"). I was taken aback by the question and upset by its inherent assumptions. *My boss thinks I'm qualified*, I wanted to scream at the firing line, *do you sign my checks?* The query angered me for a number of reasons, not the least of which was this: I didn't know that I *was* qualified. Full disclosure: I'm not even half black. My mother is of German descent and my father is part black and part American Indian, an ethnic pairing appearing in my lineage thanks to a ribald ancestor who had a stint as a Buffalo Soldier. I am an amalgam, an alloy part, and at the time I didn't feel comfortable saying that to people who seemed to be hungry for a, yes, black or white answer. My skin tone and indecision were one taupe mass.

To better pick my way through this existential dilemma, I started jotting down the incidents in my life that have made me feel truly, unshakably African American. Soon, I had composed what I hope you will indulge me enough to read, a very general glimpse into what I believe to be my "blackness," the credentials that explain my employment at a site devoted to black culture.

Cord Jefferson, "Cord Asks, Am I Black Enough for Ya?" Stereohyped.com, March 28, 2008. Reproduced by permission. http://www.stereohyped.com/cord-asks-am-i-black -enough-for-ya-20080328.

Defining Blackness

I hate *lessons*, but if I learned anything from this particular creative process, it's that though I am not by birth an archetypal African American, I have been presumed to be and treated as such, for better or worse, many, many times over the course of my history. I learned that my black experience can't be spoken of in terms of black and white. It's red like anger, green like envy, an energetic yellow and, far too often, a deep, dark blue.

I hope that no matter what color you are you'll be able to relate to at least some of the following, especially the bad parts. As I've come to know, the worst of times are almost always the most enlightening.

1985

My mother and father stand with me in front of a mirror and let me take in the differences of our tiered bodies and their varied shapes and shades. Though now my parents tell me I had been enthralled with the exercise, I do not remember it. Every time the story comes up I wonder if it had any effect on me at all.

1989

Having grown too old to continue being groomed at home, my mom takes me out for a haircut. "They'll better know how to do your hair where we're going," she assures me when I ask why we're driving past all the barbers to whom my friends go. I don't understand what she means until we finally arrive at Al's Barbershop. My mother's is the only white face in the place.

1990

In an argument on the playground at recess, a boy shouts at me, "You're never going to be nice and white like your mom!" I am left reeling with the most profound hurt I have ever experienced. It is my introduction to the notion that the color contrast between my mother and me was considered by some to be a bad thing, and that, comparatively, my skin was worse.

The Census this year puts the black population of my hometown, Tucson, Arizona, at just below three percent.

1994

A classmate with whom I periodically clash finally un-leashes it one day before school: "n-----." There is no vitriol in his voice. In fact, his tone suggests it might be a question— "Are you one?" Reflexively, I become enraged and lunge to hit him, but he runs away. When he and I are later summoned to the administration office to explain our fight, I speak first and tell the assistant principal the truth about why I had been so angry. Her mouth is still agape when I notice on her desk a picture of her blue-eyed daughter in a loving embrace with a tall black man. I am dismissed, but the other boy stays.

Sundry quotes gathered from 1996–2000 (high school)

- "Since your hair's so curly are your pubes straight?"

- "Your hair is so cute." [*Ed Note: This goes on for years*]

- From a white kid: "F--- you, you black bastard."

- From a black kid: "F--- you, you punk-ass white boy."

- "You're different from other black guys."

- "Hey, black ass!" - After the release of *Half Baked*

- "Can I touch your hair?" [*Ed Note: Again, for years*]

2000

The college I attend is 80 percent white. A good friend of mine later tells me that, when he and I first met, he assumed I was on the football team.

2001

I join a predominately white fraternity and date some white schoolmates. Soon thereafter, I hear I've gotten a nick-name among the black students: Incognegro.

2003

A white co-ed I'm dating goes home to North Carolina for Easter. While showing her grandparents photos of college, they come across a picture of her and me. "What's his race?" her grandmother asks. "He's part black, part Indian and half white," says my girlfriend. "Is he your boyfriend?" asks the aging southern belle. "I guess so," my girlfriend replies, "but he and I argue a lot." "Maybe it's that black part," her grandmother posits. This conversation takes place in a car on the way to church. The family is very religious.

My girlfriend and I are in her car talking in a parking lot in the historic district of my college town, when a security guard pulls up to the driver's side door and asks us if we know we're trespassing. We say we do not and that we'll go, but he tells my girlfriend to step out of the car and meet him back by the trunk. I'm nervous, even though I know I've done nothing wrong. The radio is on, but the music is faint enough for me to hear the guard when he asks, "Are you all right? Are you here against your will?" I jump out of the passenger seat and scream, "Did you just ask her if she was all right?" "It's common procedure, sir," the white officer tells me, holding out his hand like a lion tamer does a stool. "Now I'll ask *you*: Are *you* here against *your* will?"

In a McDonald's in Italy at four in the morning with several of my friends, a swarthy Italian puffs his chest out at us and screams, "F--- *Ame-dee-kah!*" Then, to me, "F--- *nay-gro!*" The war in Iraq is brand new and my friends and I are very obviously from "the evil empire." This is the first time I am unscathed by racism. It's the first time I personally see a racial slur as anger, not prejudice. I pity him and empathize with his disappointment in America. And I'm not about to be offended by a guy who can't see the incongruity of buying a Big Mac while railing against the US.

2004

A white girl, tall but so literally tipsy she looks half a foot shorter, lingers around my bedroom after a party at my house. She tells me she's just transferred to my college from Ole Miss. Awkward conversationalist that I am, I ask her if it's very racist there. "No," she snorts, "but what do you care? You're not even black." *What do you mean?* my expression demands. "Look at you," she says, "you're in a Polo shirt and chinos. And listen to the way you talk!" I say nothing as she continues to sway. "She's so f---ing wasted," her sorority sister tells me.

The night I graduate from college, one of my close white friends gets into a shouting match with a black graduate. I break up the argument and am walking away when the black guy grabs my arm. "Thanks a lot, *brother*," he spits. "Oh, wait, I forgot: you're a white boy." I don't know how, but I could tell he'd been waiting to say that since we were freshmen.

2005

When I ask him if he wants to rent *Do the Right Thing*, my first roommate in Los Angeles, a producer by trade, notes, "I don't watch Spike Lee movies; I can't relate to that shit."

The image-centric people of LA frequently ask me this: "What's your ethnicity?" Sometimes they say, "It's a great mix."

2007

It's my first week in New York and a black youth in baggy jeans shoves a smaller, older white commuter who has bumped into him on the L train. "Watch where the f--- you going, fag-got," the younger man screams. He stands on his toes to better tower over the white guy who is unabashedly begging for forgiveness. A small Asian woman close to the scuffle turns her head away in fright and stares at me: another tall, young black man. My face feels hot for the rest of the train ride.

2008

I begin editing at Stereohyped, where I'm asked point blank, "Cord, are you black?" I'm not sure it's anyone's business, but, yeah, I think I am. I'm also so much more.

Mixed Marriages Enrich Rather than Dilute Culture

Josh Freedman Berthoud

Many British immigrants and their descendants fear that once they or their kids marry outside their communities, their cultural heritage will be diluted. But the author, born to a Jewish father and a Christian mother, doesn't share these fears. Instead he feels that growing up with a mixed heritage can enrich you and teach you to respect other cultures and traditions. Josh Freedman Berthoud is a writer and journalist.

Despite my general indifference to the ongoing inquest into [Princess] Diana's death, the revelation that her mother had called her a "whore" for dating Muslim men struck me as an usually outdated attitude towards mixed relationships.

Perhaps my perspective has been distorted by growing up in north London, a diverse area, where ethnic mixing is widespread and common. Nevertheless, I am not used to hearing people from the white, British mainstream being so disapproving of mixed marriage; indeed, it is such a common occurrence that it has established itself as a mainstream custom, with most in the cultural centre of society accepting it as such. Thus, while many might still share her view, Frances Shand Kydd's comments jarred because they are no longer socially acceptable.

Interestingly though, it often seems to be only the cultural mainstream that approves of intermarriage, whereas people of many ethnic and religious minorities can be the most vocal in their calls to keep it in the faith/creed/colour/caste. The truth of this was made clear to me when I took part in the BBC World Service programme, World Have Your Say, on this very subject. While there were one or two instances of white people who had forbidden their offspring from dating black people, the vast majority of callers were people from ethnic minorities living in western countries, whose families had a problem with their decision to marry outside their community.

Marrying Outside One's Community

As a Jew, I am well aware of the pressures put on people not to "marry out". The other guest on the show, Sonia Ali, a Bangladeshi woman, spoke of the pressure that many Bangladeshi people feel not to marry someone outside their community. She also mentioned the derogatory Bengali word used to describe white people—"gora"—which is not dissimilar in sound to the word we Jews use to describe anyone who isn't Jewish: "goy". This is the least offensive of several synonyms, which roughly translates as one from another nation. Comparing Sonia's anecdotes with my own experiences, as well as with the numerous other stories I heard on the show, it was evident that while mainstream, white British culture might have come to accept mixed marriages as the norm, British minorities are frequently far more resistant to marrying outside the fold.

On many levels, this is understandable, and although it flies in the face of modern Britain's liberal values, I have a degree of sympathy with this view. First of all, minorities are, by definition, in the minority and tend to identify themselves, and be identified, in contrast to the mainstream majority. As preceding generations have battled to mark out this sphere of identity, they want to ensure that it is not simply lost, or swallowed up, by the next generation, as they assimilate into the dominant culture. Likewise, when religion is involved, not only are people often sceptical about the chances of partners from different faiths being able to bridge the divide, but also communities fear that the religion, customs, culture and values they have instilled into their children will be lost, or worse, rejected, in the face of a more dominant partner. As a Jew, I have frequently heard the rather emotionally-charged warning that to marry out is to complete Hitler's work for him: "We haven't come this far only for you to willingly destroy your heritage."

Destroying or Enriching Heritage?

And yet I myself am a product of a "mixed marriage" (though my parents never actually married). While my mum converted and I have been raised fully Jewish, I am grateful for my mixed heritage. After my parents' separation, and my mum's eventual rejection of religion, I enjoyed a peculiarly asymmetrical upbringing. One weekend I would spend with my dad, staying in on Shabbat, attending Synagogue, studying Talmud after a traditional lunch and then laying Tefillin [religious accessories] on Sunday morning. Then I'd spend the following weekend at my mum's, raving [partying] on Friday night before a long shop at Brent Cross on Saturday. Over the "festive season" I would speed from lighting the Hannukah candles at my dad's house to my mum's place, to hang the Christmas lights. At Easter I would hoard my eggs until the festival of Pesach's [Passover's] strict kosher laws had expired and I could eat them all.

Far from confusing me, I felt lucky that both of these elements were intrinsic to my growing identity. Many Jews I know, despite being fully assimilated into society, feel a stark divide between themselves and the prevalent, mainstream British culture. Meanwhile, many in the white, non-Jewish, British majority can't understand the Jewish community's perceived detachment and collective mindset. I, on the other hand, feel quite at home on both sides of the "divide" and I expect that many who are the product of mixed marriages, from whichever cultures, feel the same way. As a mixed race friend used to say when people called him half caste, "I'm not half, I'm double."

At the same time, however, I feel I have been born with an innate, healthy inclination to question absolute truths. For, every time that I decorated the Christmas tree, I felt my dad was there, watching. And whenever I went to shul [synagogue], there was my mum, not quite understanding. And that split sense of acting while simultaneously observing and questioning my actions—with an inherent knowledge of the other side—has stayed with me, and become an invaluable part of my constitution. Even as I feel I belong fully to the British mainstream as well as to the Jewish minority, I have the privilege of being able to sit on the peripheries of each circle and look in with an awareness of what is going on elsewhere. I apologise if that sounds a little pretentious, and certainly it is not so significant that it dominates my every waking moment, but if I am to put it into words, this is how it sounds.

Doubling the Culture and Heritage

I don't pretend that it is easy for people in mixed marriages to work out how to raise their children nor do I ignore the fact they will often have to make serious sacrifices in what they pass down. Equally, I would be lying if I said it didn't bother me whether I raise my children to be Jewish. It does, and I fully understand people's need not only to continue what their family and community have preserved, but also to give their children the heritage that they themselves treasure.

However, mixed marriages have their own benefits, and as long as parents can work out a way to pass down both sets of cultures and values, then the birth of their offspring needn't mark the end or dilution of their heritage, but in fact a doubling of it (with the added bonus of having children with a natural inclination to question everything they're told). So, while many minorities may still be as resistant to intermarriage as Diana's anachronistic mother, I would urge them to think not of what they will lose, but instead of what they could gain when "one of their own" marries one of somebody else's.

The Power of Words

Wei Ming Dariotis

Being of Chinese, Greek, Swedish, English, Scottish, and German ancestry, the author struggles to find an identity until she adopts the word Hapa. Hapa, *originally a Hawaiian term used to describe people of mixed Hawaiian and non-Hawaiian heritage, has come to define people of mixed Asian descent. But after years of defining herself through that word, she realized that the new use has robbed* Hapa *of its true meaning and taken identity away from its original members. She begins a quest to find a new term to do justice to her heritage. Wei Ming Dariotis is assistant professor of Asian American studies at San Francisco State University.*

The poet Truong Tran told me that when he was a young boy his Tolkiensian "ring of power" was the English word "f--k." This word made him American; it was like a secret language, something his parents didn't speak, a word of his own. He used it gleefully, like Bilbo used the ring, to set himself above where he had been. Eventually, like Frodo, Tran had to destroy the ring before it would destroy him. Tran accomplished this by writing his book of poetry, *Within the Margin*.

My ring of power was also a word, the word "Hapa." I first learned this word in 1992, when I was 23 years old. I was a second-year English Literature doctoral student at UC [University of California] Santa Barbara, and I was enrolled in the course, "The World of Amerasians," taught by Teresa K. Williams. When I learned the word "Hapa" I felt as though a whole new world had opened up to me. Before this, when anybody asked me, "What are you?" I had to answer, "Chinese Greek Swedish English Scottish German Pennsylvania Dutch."

Wei Ming Dariotis, "Hapa: The Word of Power," MixedHeritageCenter.org, December 3, 2007. Reproduced by permission. http://www.mixedheritagecenter.org/index.php ?option=com_content&task=view&id=1259&Itemid=1.

This was a list of my ancestry. It is my heritage. However, this list is not my identity. Heritage does not equal identity. To paraphrase the title of the book on Asian Americans of mixed heritage edited by Teresa K. Williams and Cynthia Nakashima, my identity is something more than the sum of my parts. "Hapa" gave me such an identity. Instead of worrying, "where am I going to find another Chinese Greek Swedish English Scottish German Pennsylvania Dutch American?" I realized I already had a Hapa community.

Finding an Identity

The word "Hapa" made me something more than just a half Chinese or a fake Filipino. When I joined the board of the Asian American Theater Company, I fulfilled the need for diversity in terms of being Hapa despite the fact that most of the other board members at that time were Chinese—and so am I. When I joined the faculty of the Department of Asian American studies at San Francisco State University, I also fulfilled their need for a mixed heritage Asian American. In fact, the position I occupy, as far as I know the first one in the US so described, is for a specialist in Asian Americans of mixed heritage. For reports from the various ethnic units in our department, I am not counted among the Chinese American faculty, rather, I am referred to as the Hapa unit, or to paraphrase the Eurasian writer, Diana Chang, "The Hapa Contingent."

Of course, the years I worked with Hapa Issues Forum were the height of the power of the word *Hapa* for me. In particular, I recall a leadership retreat in which two remarkable things happened. The first was simple, and nobody planned it: throughout the entire weekend, among the more than 30 people present, I never heard anyone ask anyone else, "What are you?" I find this remarkable because it is actually quite common for mixed heritage people to ask each other about their ethnic heritage—we are often trying to find points of commonality, but sometimes we are just competing a little bit to find out who has the longest list. What struck me during this weekend, was the fact that the 30 of us may have shared almost no common ethnic heritages, but for that weekend it did not matter; we were all Hapa. We were part of a larger community. The other thing that happened was planned by our executive director, Sheila Chung. Sheila, who is Argentinean and Korean, led us on a visioning exercise that I have never forgotten. Sitting around a campfire, we were instructed to close our eyes and envision the earth below us while we hovered above in the sky. Slowly we descended through the clouds and we could see a landscape below us. Within this landscape was a building; a sign on the building read, "Hapa Culture Center." Within the building there was a library stocked with books about Asian Americans of mixed heritage, an art gallery for art by Asian Americans of mixed heritage, a theater for gatherings and performances, a space for an after-school program and a summer camp, and meeting rooms.

Finding a Place

We never built that building, or have not yet built it. Hapa Issues Forum as an organization lasted only from 1992 to 2004. Yet the word "Hapa" in many ways has been that building for me and many other mixed heritage Asian Americans. It has given us a space of our own, a place where we can be us, without having to explain ourselves. Anyone entering the space created by the word accepts our identity. In this way it works opposite from Bilbo and Frodo's ring of power, which makes the wearer invisible; the word "Hapa" makes my community visible, that is its power.

However, power, as we all know, always creates the seeds of its own destruction. The very success of the word "Hapa" has been in some ways its downfall. What I mean to say is that the word "Hapa" as it is used now can never go back to what it (or what "hapa") once meant: a Native Hawaiian word meaning mixed or part or half, as in the phrase "hapa haole." This phrase means part European American, with the implication being that the person is also part Native Hawaiian. In Hawaii there are other kinds of hapa people. You will notice that I'm not capitalizing the word when I use it in its Native Hawaiian context. I am also not using the term here like an ethnic signifier, which is what the word "Hapa" has become in the mainland context. In contrast, the native Hawaiian word is an adjective. Increasingly, many Native Hawaiian people object not only to the way the word has been changed in its grammatical usage, but also to how it is applied to anyone of mixed Asian and or Pacific Islander heritage, when it implies Native Hawaiian mixed heritage. This is not merely a question of trying to hold on to a word that like many words encountered in the English language has been adopted, assimilated, or appropriated. This is a question of power. Who has the power or right to use language? Native Hawaiians, in addition to all of the other ways that their sovereignty has been abrogated, lost for many years the right to their own language through oppressive English-language education. Given this history and given the contemporary social and political reality (and realty—as in real estate) of Hawaiian, Japanese Americans and other Asian American ethnic groups that numerically and economically dominate Native Hawaiians in their own land. . . .

There is a website called www.realhapas.com, on which Lana Robbins states, "When Hawaiians began to mix with Caucasians they began to have offspring who were Hawaiian and Caucasian. That is when Hawaiians of Hawaiian and Caucasian ancestry created a Hawaiian word to describe themselves and people like them. Eventually these Hawaiians of Hawaiian and Caucasian ancestry began to use the word 'hapa' for a part, portion, or fragment of Hawaiian people, places, and things. Until [Japanese Americans] began to rape their language. Today's rape of the Hawaiian language also implies that the Hawaiian language means nothing and thus the Hawaiian people are nothing."

Robbins continues, "The raping of Hawaii continues with a new group of Colonizers, the California Wanna Be Hapas. As colonizers, California Wanna Be Hapas raped from Hawaiian Hapas their very identity, culture, and history and called it their own. These colonizers justified their illegal actions by creating organizations such as Hapa Issues Forum and other 'Hapa' online forums. They gained allies from elite mixed Eurasians who like California Wanna Be Hapas, stole their term from the wartime and colonial Eurasians while stomping on the rights of Amerasians and Hawaiian Hapas."

The Power of Words

My response to first hearing this protest was to say, "But I like the word 'Hapa'; look at everything it has done for us." I didn't want to give "Hapa" up. I remember how hard it was just to get people to use it. When I first started to use the word in 1992, I encountered Korean, Chinese and Filipino people of mixed heritage who objected to using the word "Hapa" because they thought it was a Japanese term. They didn't want to feel colonized by the Japanese language the way their ancestors had been colonized by Japan. When I informed these people that the word was Native Hawaiian in origin, they gladly adopted it for themselves. Native Hawaiians have never colonized anyone. Besides, most mixed Asians are mistaken for being Hawaiian—and there is a certain glamour in being associated with the islands. Like many of us, I have been frequently told, "You must be from some exotic island somewhere!" (I had long hair at the time. I cut it.)

When criticism against Asian Americans using the term "Hapa" first started being raised strongly in 2002, I realized that the fact that Native Hawaiians had never colonized anyone, and that is therefore why mixed heritage Asian Americans feel comfortable to use the word, was a sign of the relative power of Asian Americans in this context. Maybe the word "Hapa" was a colonizing violence in which I was participating. At a 2003 talk at UC Berkeley I mentioned my increasing concerns about using the word "Hapa." I was very surprised when a young man in the audience became visibly upset at the suggestion that the word "Hapa" might be somehow taken away from him. It meant so much to him for the same reasons it meant so much to me—it provides a sense of community and identity in one simple word.

In other words, quite possibly, the word "Hapa," which I had been so happy to wear because of the sense of identity and community it gave me, might have to be destroyed—or like Frodo's ring, which was forged in the fires of Mt. Doom, returned to the point of origin to be destroyed or at least reshaped. I say this knowing that the word can never be again what it once was. There is a nostalgia here that cannot be satisfied even if everyone were to stop using the word "Hapa" to refer to non-Native Hawaiian mixed Asians. But while I certainly do not have the power to fling this word into a 'Mt. Doom' of linguistic destruction, I do feel responsible to participate in the dialogue. I have been silent on this issue for too long, perhaps hoping that it would go away, so I could keep "my" word.

The controversy has not gone away, it has only grown stronger, and it is time for me—and other mixed heritage Asian Americans—to recognize that when we use the word "Hapa" it causes some people pain. What is so troubling about this is that the word "Hapa" was chosen because it was the only word we could find that did not really cause us pain. It is not any of the Asian words for mixed Asian people that contain negative connotations either literally (e.g., "children of the dust," "mixed animal") or by association (Eurasian). It avoids the confused identity and the Black-White dichotomy implied by English phrases (e.g., mixed blood, biracial). It was adopted to enhance an Asian-focus to our mixed identity, thereby allowing us to use the word to participate more fully in our Asian American communities—rather than being separated into the larger mixed race community (and perhaps being subsumed under the Black-White dichotomy).

Searching for a New Identity

Making a change away from using "Hapa" will be a steep uphill struggle. Aside from the growing usage of the word both within and beyond the Asian American and mixed-heritage communities, the word is featured in the titles of such publications as Marie Hara and Nora Okja-Keller's anthology, *Intersecting Circles: The Voices of Hapa Women in Poetry and Prose*; Kip Fulbeck's photo book, *Part Asian 100% Hapa*; and the recently published memoir by May-Lee Chai, *Hapa Girl*. Where does that leave us? Is it too late to stem the tide? Languages grow and evolve, and how they do so reveals the traces of power—but is it our lot to merely record and uncover those changes? Or is it our responsibility to shape those changes? I have to acknowledge that, through my work with Hapa Issues Forum and as a writer and an educator, I have contributed to spreading the use of the word "Hapa" by Asian Americans.

Meanwhile, Hapa Issues Forum has folded as an organization, though many still believe that there is a real need to have an organization specific to the needs of mixed heritage Asian Americans (it focuses on issues specific to the Asian American community, outside of the Black-White binary oppositional racial dialogue, and it provides mixed heritage Asian Americans a venue in which to be authentically Asian American). The Hapa Clubs that had started on so many college campuses in the late 1990s and early 2000s have mostly abandoned this term in favor of more general mixed heritage inclusion: Berkeley's Mixed Student Union, Variations (UCSB—formerly VariAsians and SFSU—formerly the Hapa Club), Fusion (Wellesly), Half and Half (Bryn Mawr), Students of Mixed Heritage (Amherst), The Biracial and Multiracial Student Association (NYU), The Multiracial Identified Community (Stanford), Multiracial and Biracial Student Association (University of Maryland), Check One (University of Pennsylvania), and MiXed (University of Washington). Cornell Hapa Student Association, Harvard HAPA (Half Asian People's Association), and the UCLA Hapa Club retain the term "Hapa." Communities and the language that represents them change quickly, and redefine themselves even before you have a chance to write them into history.

I presented an earlier version of this paper on November 15th, 2007, at a talk at Occidental College. At the end of my two hours of sharing my research and my poetry—which included a series of "Hapa Poems" written mostly around 2002–2005—a young woman, who identified herself as Native Hawaiian and Japanese American, told me that my use of the word "Hapa" felt like a violence—like something was being taken away from her—another piece of Hawaii, another piece of Native Hawaiian culture and identity. She reminded me that I am part of this problem, that I am responsible and have influence and power in this dialogue. She was right. So here is the first step—my first attempt to send the word of power into the fire, to be re-forged to serve the community for which it was originally intended—people of mixed Native Hawaiian heritage. A word used to give power to one community, while taking power away from another, is not a word I can use in good conscience. However, I will still slip up, I will still say "Hapa" to mean people like me the way I still sometimes use sexist language despite 20 years of trying to train myself not to, but I will not read my "Hapa Poems" any more until I can find a way to elegantly revise them [Laura Kina kindly reminds me that perhaps I should simply recognize that these are the works of a particular time period, rather than trying to revise all of my former work to meet a new standard], and I will not use "Hapa" anymore in my academic writings as a shorthand for Asian Americans of mixed heritage.

Leaving "Hapa" Behind

What to replace it with? We could switch from using "Hapa" to using "Asian Americans of mixed heritage," which is the title of the class I teach at San Francisco State. The problem is that it is much harder to rally around the "mixed heritage Asian American community" than it was to be part of the Hapa Club. But it is for other reasons that I am growing uncomfortable with using the term "mixed heritage," which has always seemed something of a stop-gap measure. It is meant to be inclusive of transracial adoptees as well as those who are of mixed ethnicity (who must deal with ethnic hierarchies within racialized groups), but then it seems to elide what is still the main issue in our society—race. Jayne Ifekwunigwe makes a good argument, in her introduction to *'Mixed Race' Studies: A Reader*, for using 'mixed race' in quotation marks rather than "mixed heritage"—because "mixed heritage" can be so easily co-opted—who is not, to some extent, of "mixed heritage"? Furthermore, as I mentioned earlier, heritage does not equal identity, and "Hapa" was for me an identity that conveyed community.

It was Marlon Hom, as Chair of Asian American Studies at SFSU, who set up the course I teach and named it "Asian Americans of Mixed Heritage," not "Hapa Studies," though this is what many people regularly call it. It was also he who recently suggested maybe we should change the name because "mixed heritage" does not quite seem to satisfy. Ah, but to what? Multiple Identity Asian Americans?—That raises the specter of split personalities, which of course is a common stereotype of us. Manifold Community Association Asian Americans? Asian Americans Plus? I am drawn to the image of the Venn Diagram implied by the title *Intersecting Circles*, but while that makes a great visual to describe how we can and do maintain allegiances to multiple communities and identities, it isn't a great label (Venn Asian Americans?). I hate to say this, but "Hapa" has great mouth feel as a word, until the bad taste of Native Hawaiian oppression slips in. My talents as a wordsmith do not extend to creating new language whole cloth, with no negative connotations, so, for now, this essay is only the first stage in the anti-colonial project of refusing to mis-use the word "Hapa." Stage two will be coming up with a new word that encompasses mixed heritage Asians and Pacific Islanders, without coming from a dominating or oppressed language. I feel a little bit like an advertising executive, being asked to avoid another Chevy Nova fiasco.[1] Calling all poets—we've got to be able to come up with something good, short, and catchy—that's the challenge. My dear friend, Dr. Marianne Maruyama Halpin, reminded me, after reading this essay, that "A name, to work, needs to be something loved." With that in mind let us find a name we can all love calling ourselves and that also causes no one else pain.

1. Chevrolet tried to market its Chevy Nova model in Latin America until the company recognized that "No-va" in Spanish means "it does not go."

Organizations to Contact

The editors have compiled the following list of organizations concerned with the issues debated in this book. The descriptions are derived from materials provided by the organizations. All have publications or information available for interested readers. The list was compiled on the date of publication of the present volume; the information provided here may change. Be aware that many organizations take several weeks or longer to respond to inquiries, so allow as much time as possible.

Adopted and Fostered Adults of the African Diaspora (AFAAD)
PO Box 24771, Oakland, CA 94607
e-mail: afaadinfo@gmail.com
Web site: http://afaad.wordpress.com/

AFAAD works to ensure that conversations around adoption in both academia and in general society progress in a way that includes contributions by adult adoptees. The organization supports those who are conducting cutting-edge research, restructuring child welfare laws and policies, and creating new artwork, performance, and films. Articles and blogs are available on its Web site.

Association of MultiEthnic Americans (AMEA)
PO Box 29223, Los Angeles, CA 90029-0223
e-mail: info@ameasite.org
Web site: www.ameasite.org

AMEA is an international association of organizations dedicated to advocacy, education, and collaboration on behalf of the multiethnic, multiracial, and transracial adoption community. Articles on these subjects are available on its Web site.

Interracial Family Circle (IFC)
4923 E. Chalk Point Road, West River, MD   20778
e-mail: info@interracialfamilycircle.org
Web site: www.interracialfamilycircle.org

Since 1984, the Interracial Family Circle has provided opportunities for the education, support, and socialization of multiracial individuals and families, people involved in interracial relationships, and transracial adoptive families in the Washington, D.C., metropolitan area. Resources and book reviews are available on its Web site.

iPride
1581 LeRoy Ave., Berkeley, CA   94708
(510) 644-1000 ext. 2 • fax: (510) 525-4106
Web site: www.ipride.org

iPride seeks to cultivate positive identity formation in children who are of more than one racial or ethnic heritage, or who have been transracially adopted. The organization strives to create a more inclusive and equitable society by educating adults, children, and communities about multiethnic families, mixed-heritage identity, and transracial adoptee experiences.

Loving Day
Web site: www.lovingday.org

Loving Day's mission is to fight prejudice through education and to build a sense of community among people who engage in meaningful interracial and intercultural relationships. Loving Day observes June 12 as "Loving Day," a celebration of the Supreme Court decision *Loving v. Virginia* that in 1967 legalized interracial marriage in the United States. Blogs and online groups can be accessed on the Web site.

MAVIN Foundation
1425 Broadway #517, Seattle, WA   98122-3854
(206) 622-7101

e-mail: contact@mavinfoundation.org
Web site: www.mavinfoundation.org

MAVIN Foundation strives to build communities that celebrate and empower mixed-heritage people and families. Its projects explore the experiences of mixed-heritage people, transracial adoptees, interracial relationships, and multiracial families. Together with the Association of MultiEthnic Americans (AMEA), the organization launched the Mixed Heritage Center, a national clearinghouse of information related to mixed-heritage and transracial adoption issues. MAVIN publishes a magazine of the same name.

Mixed Roots Movement/MixedRoots Projects

PO Box 250045, Franklin, MI 48025
e-mail: info@mixedrootsmovement.info
Web site: www.mixedrootsmovement.info

MixedRoots provides resources and education to help create communities that celebrate and respect racial and religious diversity. Mixed Roots Movement and the MixedRoots projects aim to explore, educate, challenge perceptions, and provide a place for the mixed-race community to celebrate their heritages and unions and share their experiences. Resources and articles can be accessed on its Web site.

Swirl

(212) 561-1773
e-mail: info@swirlinc.org
Web site: www.swirlinc.org

Swirl is a national multiethnic organization seeking to challenge society's notions of race through community building, education, and action. Videos and articles can be accessed on its Web site.

The Topaz Club (TTC)

Web site: www.thetopazclub.com

TTC is a social-support sisterhood for biracial/multiracial women of African/African American descent who are mixed with other heritages. TTC exists to serve as a professional, social, and support network for it members. It also addresses issues that affect multiracial women of African/African American descent. The Topaz Club operates as an online community and has chapters in select cities around the United States.

For Further Research

Books

Suki Ali, *Mixed-Race, Post-Race: Gender, New Ethnicities and Cultural Practices.* Oxford, UK: Berg, 2003.

Yasmin Alibhai-Brown, *Mixed Feelings: The Complex Lives of Mixed-Race Britons.* London: Women's Press, 2001.

Wanni Wibulswasdi Anderson and Robert Lee, *Displacements and Diasporas: Asians in the Americas.* New Brunswick, NJ: Rutgers University Press, 2005.

Kwame Anthony Appiah, *The Ethics of Identity.* Princeton, NJ: Princeton University Press, 2004.

Zygmunt Bauman, *Liquid Modernity.* Cambridge, UK: Polity Press, 2000.

Ben Bradford, *Who Are the 'Mixed' Ethnic Group?* London: Office for National Statistics, 2006.

Heather Dalmadge, *Tripping on the Color Line: Black-White Multiracial Families in a Racially Divided World.* New Brunswick, NJ: Rutgers University Press, 2000.

G. Reginald Daniel, *More than Black? Multiracial Identity and the New Racial Order.* Philadelphia: Temple University Press, 2001.

Peter Feng, *Screening Asian Americans.* New Brunswick, NJ: Rutgers University Press, 2002.

Joan Ferrante and Prince Browne Jr., *The Social Construction of Race and Ethnicity in the United States.* 2nd ed. Upper Saddle River, NJ: Prentice Hall, 2001.

Timothy Fong and Larry H. Shinagawa, *Asian-Americans: Experiences and Perspectives.* Upper Saddle River, NJ: Prentice Hall, 2000.

Kip Fulbeck, *Part Asian, 100% Hapa*. San Francisco: Chronicle Books, 2006.

Lawrence Hill, *Black Berry, Sweet Juice: On Being Black and White in Canada*. Toronto: HarperFlamingo, 2001.

Eric Yo Ping Lai and Dennis Arguelles, *The New Face of Asian Pacific America: Numbers, Diversity and Change in the 21st Century*. San Francisco: AsianWeek, with UCLA's Asian American Studies Center Press, in cooperation with the Organization of Chinese Americans and the National Coalition for Asian Pacific American Community Development, 2003; Torrance, CA: Frank Schaffer, 2003.

Pyong Gap Min, *The Second Generation: Ethnic Identity Among Asian Americans*. Walnut Creek, CA: AltaMira Press, 2002.

Phyl Newbeck, *Virginia Hasn't Always Been for Lovers: Interracial Marriage Bans and the Case of Richard and Mildred Loving*. Carbondale: Southern Illinois University Press, 2004.

Gary Okihiro, *The Columbia Guide to Asian American History*. New York: Columbia University Press, 2001.

J. Olumide, *Raiding the Gene Pool: The Social Construction of Mixed Race*. London: Pluto, 2002.

Maria Root and Matt Kelley, eds., *The Multiracial Child Resource Book*, Mavin Foundation, 2003.

Maria Root and Matt Kelley, eds., *Love's Revolution: Interracial Marriage*. Philadelphia: Temple University Press, 2001.

Tommie Shelby, *We Who Are Dark: The Philosophical Foundations of Black Solidarity*. Cambridge, MA: Belknap Press, 2005.

Linda Trinh Võ and Rick Bonus, *Contemporary Asian American Communities: Intersections and Divergences*. Philadelphia: Temple University Press, 2002.

Rebecca Walker, *Black, White, and Jewish: Autobiography of a Shifting Self*. Riverhead Books, 2000.

Peter Wallenstein, *Tell the Court I Love My Wife: Race, Marriage, and Law; An American History*. New York: Palgrave, 2002.

Teresa Williams-Leon and Cynthia Nakashima, eds., *The Sum of Our Parts: Mixed-Heritage Asian Americans*. Philadelphia: Temple University Press, 2001.

Deborah Woo, *Glass Ceilings and Asian Americans: The New Face of Workplace Barriers*. Walnut Creek, CA: AltaMira Press, 2000.

Periodicals

Robin Andreasen, "Race: Biological Reality or Social Construct?" *British Journal of the Philosophy of Science*, 2000.

Michael Bamshad and Steve Olson, "Does Race Exist?" *Scientific American*, December 2003.

Herb Boyd, "Racism Persists as Progress Is Made," *New York Amsterdam News*, August 2, 2001.

Eamonn Callon, "The Ethics of Assimilation," *Ethics*, 2005.

Sapna Cheryan and Benoît Monin, "'Where Are You Really From?': Asian Americans and Identity Denial," *Journal of Personality and Social Psychology*, November 2005.

Jeff Chu, Nadia Mustafa, Kristin Kloberdanz, and Amanda Bower, "Between Two Worlds," *Time*, January 16, 2006.

Daily Mail (London), "Mixed-Race Britain, 2005," March 22, 2005.

Daily Mail (London), "Rapid Rise of Mixed-Race Britons," January 22, 2007.

Arnold Dashefsky, "Double or Nothing? Jewish Families and Mixed Marriage," *American Jewish History*, March 2004.

Clare Davidson, "Race Relations in Brazil: Deciding Who Is Really Black," *New Statesman*, June 28, 2004.

Amitai Etzioni, "Leaving Race Behind: Our Growing Hispanic Population Creates a Golden Opportunity," *American Scholar*, Spring 2006.

Anne Fisher, "Piercing the 'Bamboo Ceiling,'" *Fortune*, August 22, 2005.

E.J. Graff, "Divided to the Vein: A Journey into Race and Family," *American Prospect*, September 10, 2001.

Kara Joyner and Grace Kao, "Interracial Relationships and the Transition to Adulthood," *American Sociological Review*, August 2005.

Oona King, "We All Have Dual Heritage Somewhere," *New Statesman*, August 7, 2006.

Tru Leverette, "Traveling Identities: Mixed Race Quests and Fran Ross's Oreo," *African American Review*, March 2006.

Michael Levin, "The Race Concept: A Defense," *Behavior and Philosophy*, 2002.

Pei-te Lien, M. Margaret Conway, and Janelle Wong, "The Contours and Sources of Ethnic Identity Choices Among Asian Americans," *Social Science Quarterly*, June 2003.

Lydia Lum, "Stepping Forward," *Diverse: Issues in Higher Education*, August 25, 2005.

S. McCarthy, "Mixed Race," *New African*, February 2005.

Enuma Okoro, "Race and Romance," *Christian Century*, November 14, 2006.

Steve Olson, "The Genetic Archaeology of Race," *Atlantic Monthly*, April 2001.

Carina Ray, "The Origins of Mixed Race Populations," *New African*, January 2005.

Ronald R. Sundstrom, "Being and Being Mixed Race," *Social Theory and Practice*, April 2001.

Margaret Connell Szasz, "'Real' Indians and Others: Mixed-Blood Urban Native Peoples and Indigenous Nationhood," *American Review of Canadian Studies*, December 2005.

Lowri Turner, "Why I Have Mixed Feelings About My Mixed Race Baby," *Daily Mail* (London), July 12, 2007.

Washington Times, "Three Percent of Americans Are Mixed-Race; Census Study Is First of Its Kind," April 8, 2005.

Index